ROYAL PRIES

Ye are an elect race, a royal priesthood, a holy nation, a people for God's own possession, that ye may shew forth the excellencies of him who called you out of darkness into his marvellous light.

1 Peter 2.9

ROYAL PRIESTHOOD

A Theology of Ordained Ministry

T. F. TORRANCE

Second Edition

T&T CLARK
EDINBURGH

T&T CLARK LTD
59 GEORGE STREET
EDINBURGH EH2 2LQ
SCOTLAND

www.tandtclark.co.uk

First edition 1955
Second edition 1993
Latest impression 1999

ISBN 0 567 29222 3

British Library Cataloguing-in-Publication Data
A catalogue record for this book is available
from the British Library

Printed and bound in Great Britain by MPG Books Ltd, Bodmin

To the CHURCH OF ENGLAND, the church of
  my mother and my wife, and
to the CHURCH OF SCOTLAND, the church of
  my father,
in the earnest prayer that they may soon
  be one

CONTENTS

		PAGE
	Preface	ix
I.	THE ROYAL PRIEST	1
II.	THE FUNCTION OF THE BODY OF CHRIST	23
III.	THE TIME OF THE CHURCH	43
IV.	THE PRIESTHOOD OF THE CHURCH	63
V.	THE CORPORATE EPISCOPATE	88

PREFACE

This book was first published in the aftermath of the Faith and Order Conference at Lund in 1952 when sustained theological consideration was given to the doctrine of the Church as the Body of Christ and to organic union between churches, which while diverse in their order are nevertheless united through the one Baptism common to Christ and his Church. It was during this period that the Church of Scotland and the Church of England engaged in talks on reunion in the hope of finding a way to bring together episcopacy and presbytery on a Christological basis which called for a rethinking of the nature of priesthood. This essay, first published as *Occasional Paper* No. 3 of the *Scottish Journal of Theology* in 1955, was offered as a contribution to those discussions with a view to bringing into the centre the Biblical and Patristic approach to the understanding of the evangelical and catholic ministry of the Church as a Royal Priesthood, participating by way of service in the Priesthood of the Lord Jesus Christ, who is the one Mediator between God and mankind (1 Tim 2.5).

In recent years the nature of the ministry as a priesthood has been raised in an acute way in the debates about the ministry of women in the Church of England and their ordination to the priesthood. In this connection I published a pamphlet entitled *The Ministry of Women* (Handsel Press, Edinburgh, 1992), but as it became increasingly evident that the essential nature of priesthood was being misunderstood, calls have come from people on both sides of the Atlantic for the republication of this little work.

Several years after it first appeared it came under heavy criticism from James Barr in his book *The Semantics of Biblical Language* (Oxford, 1961), not because of its presentation of the relation between the Royal Priesthood of the Church and the unique Priesthood of Christ, but because of the way in which I had used and interpreted a number of biblical terms and themes, largely under the guidance of Kittel's *Theological Dictionary of the New Testament* to which Barr was also rather hostile. Professor Barr is a brilliant philologist whose ideas cannot be ignored, although they are often rather exaggerated. His critical linguistic examination of my account of the way in which New Testament passages are to be understood in the light of the Old Testament was intended to clear away what he felt to be some serious misunderstandings of biblical teaching. Some of his criticisms I accept, but by no means all of them – in any case they do not affect at all the main thrust of the book. I believe that his basic approach and line of argument was misleading and unfortunate, for it treated language independently as something having significance in itself, to be interpreted through the interrelation of words and statements and the syntactical patterns of continuous discourse, and not primarily by reference to the realities beyond which they are meant to direct us. While this has the advantage of helping to counteract misleading subjectivist slant in interpretation, it inevitably widens the gap between language and being by reducing the semantic function of language to the syntactic relations linguistic units have with one another. This is a peculiar form of nominalism which rejects the relation of language to knowledge and culture, and which to get any kind of sense out of theological language treats it as some kind of description of religious phenomena. It is not surprising that by denigrating the objective reference of biblical language Barr should find so many biblical theologians 'obscure', for he fails by his conflation of semantics with syntactics to deal faithfully with their language in accordance with their intention in using it. He thus neglects the fundamental principle of hermeneutics advanced by the Greek Fathers that we do not subject realities to the terms referring to them, but subject terms to the realities to which they refer. The Latin Fathers followed suit with their axiom, *non sermoni res, sed rei sermo subiectus est.* This is particularly the case with biblical language for the divine truth signified lies beyond the words and statements signifying it. Hence in spite of what James Barr had to say about the biblical and theological language deployed in this book I have allowed it to appear in its original form, not because it is in no need of linguistic correction, but because I stand fully by the argument it advances and the biblical and theological truth which it attempts to set forth.

While that has to be said in a republication of this work, my interest in it is with something rather different. This is the very important matter of the nature of priesthood to which it draws attention, for the current debate seems to reflect serious misunderstanding on the part of many who reject the ordination of women and also on the part of many who want women to be ordained. On both sides of the discussion there seems to be a lapse into the erroneous idea that priesthood has to do with 'power', the 'power' with which priests are endowed in celebrating the Eucharist and in giving absolution, and does not have to do with a self-abnegating form of ministry in which it is not the priest but Christ himself who is the real Celebrant – so that like John the Baptist the priest must retreat before the presence of Christ: 'He must increase, but I must decrease' (John 3.30). What has come to the surface today, however, is the 'sacerdotalising of the priesthood' that developed after the fifth century in the teaching of the Roman Catholic Church. As the great Jesuit Liturgiologist J. A. Jungmann has shown in his revealing book *The Place of Christ in Liturgical Prayer* (London, 1965), there took place a decided shift in the worship and theology of the Church in which Christ was identified with the majesty and power of Almighty God in such a way that the conception of his vicarious human priesthood tended to fade out of the worship and theology of the Church, with the result that the poor creature was confronted immediately with the overwhelming majesty of God inducing fear in the human heart. This was reflected in the change of language from *pontifex* to *sacerdos,* that is, away from Christ regarded as a bridge in his vicarious humanity between men and women and God to Christ as an omnipotent mediator of divine gifts from God to them (Ch. 14, 'The High Priest and the Eucharist', pp. 239–263). But in that case there arose a demand for other functionaries exercising a mediatorial ministry, to make up for the human priesthood of Christ, a priesthood which could stand in for Christ, mediate between the sinner and Christ, and which was endowed with power from Christ to act on his behalf and in his place and as *sacerdos* to dispense the gifts of divine grace and blessing entrusted to the institutional Church. Along with this change came a grave misunderstanding of the saving mission of Christ and the evangelical mission of the Church, and therefore of the way in which ministry or priesthood in the Church is exercised, for a strong Pelagian element entered into the Roman conception of the eucharistic sacrifice and of the sacrificing activity of priesthood, as is very evident in the Tridentine doctrine of the sacrifice of the Roman mass.

Let me express this problem as seen through the eyes of a Greek Orthodox theologian, A. J. Philippou, who in a book called *The Orthodox Ethos* (Oxford, 1964) pointed out that the mission of Christ, which had been at the root of the division between Roman Catholics and Protestants in the sixteenth century, had long before been the central issue between the Greek Orthodox and the Roman Church. 'According to the traditional Roman Catholic view', he wrote, 'the mission of Christ is bequeathed to his disciples, giving them and their successors the authority to teach (*munus doctrinale*), to govern (*munus regale*) and to sacrifice (*munus sacerdotale*). The gift of the Holy Spirit is understood in terms of *possession*, making the *magisterium* of the Church the link between Christ and the believer. The Church becomes a divine institution (*de jure divino*), a perfect society (*societas perfecta*) with the explicit task of exercising Christ's apostolate as teacher, king and priest. This theory, which implies a denial of the *completeness* and *finality* of the unique mission of Christ, has been the ground of the debate between the Greek East and the Latin West' (p. 78f). Dr Philippou then raised what he called 'the basic question'. 'Is the Holy Spirit the endowment bequeathed by Christ to the Church, i.e. the *magisterium*, to administer his grace? In other words, is the Church subjected to God's grace, or is God's grace subjected to the activity of the clergy?' (p. 90). This question, framed in terms of the Trinitarian nature of faith and authority in the Church, was raised by Greek Orthodox theologians early in their dialogue with Reformed theologians which led to the historic *Agreed Statement on the Holy Trinity* formulated in 1991, in which the problem was traced back to an element of subordinationism in the Latin doctrine of the Trinity. (*Theological Dialogue between Orthodox and Reformed Theologians,* which I have edited, vol. 1, Edinburgh, 1985 – Vol. 2 containing the Agreed Statement is also published this year.)

A considerable change has now taken place in the Roman Catholic Church which is particularly apparent in the primacy being given to salvation history in the doctrine of the Holy Trinity and in its Christological approach to the doctrine of the Church as the Body of Christ found above all in the *Lumen Gentium* or the Dogmatic Constitution on the Church as framed in the Second Vatican Council. This is reflected in an economic and patristic understanding of the Eucharist and its celebration bringing it back into line with the conception of the human priesthood of Christ as expressed in the words 'through whom, *with* whom and in him' found in the ancient Alexandrian anaphoras and in the old Roman canon of the mass. However, this has not been translated into the Roman doctrine of the holy ministry, for the sacerdotalisation of priesthood remains entrenched and is permanently imprisoned in its codex of canon law. It was this un-Anglican sacerdotalising of the priesthood that was introduced into the Church of England through nineteenth century Tractarians in their desire to make Anglican orders acceptable to Rome, and it is still being paraded by some Anglo-Catholics as 'apostolic' and 'catholic', although it conflicts as sharply with the apostolic teaching of the ancient Catholic Church as it does with that of the Orthodox Church today.

Here, then, we have the root of the misunderstanding of priesthood by some women who feel called to the holy ministry but unfortunately clamour for 'power' enabling them to celebrate the Eucharist and to give absolution – which is far from being what priesthood and the eucharist really are about. This distorted conception derives from and reflects the sacerdotalisation of ministerial priesthood that governs those Anglo-Catholics who oppose the ordination of women and seek strangely to justify their stance on the ground that only a male can represent Christ at the Eucharist, as though the Incarnation had made no change in the order of fallen humanity in which man was held to be the head of the woman within and beyond marriage; and as though in his

Incarnation the Son of God, the Creator in whom all women and men live and move and have their being, had not assumed *all* humanity, female as well as male, in order to redeem and save them. Although Jesus was of course physically male, divine nature and human nature, divine being and human being, were perfectly and indivisibly united in his one incarnate *Person*, and it is as the incarnate *Person* of the Son of God, not as male, that he is our Lord and Saviour. And it is precisely as such, not just as male, that he, the Son of Man as Jesus spoke of himself, gives us his flesh to eat and his blood to drink (John 6.53). Moreover, the mistaken idea that it is not the priest as *person* but as *male* who can represent Christ, not only involves a form of Nestorian heresy in dividing between the divine and human natures of Christ, but conflicts sharply with the great soteriological principle of the ancient Catholic Church that 'what has not been assumed has not been saved'.

The reissue of this book today, however, does not relate specifically to the ordination of women which cannot be rejected on sound biblical or orthodox theological grounds. It is concerned rather with a re-presentation of the biblical and ancient catholic understanding of the royal priesthood of the Church incorporated into Christ as his Body, and of the priesthood of the ordained ministry of the Church in consecrated service to the Lord Jesus Christ our great High Priest who through the atoning sacrifice of himself, offered once for all for the sins of the world, has ascended to the right hand of the Father, where he continues to exercise his heavenly Priesthood in advocacy and intercession on our behalf. That is the Priesthood which is echoed through the Spirit in the corporate ministry of the Church as the Body of Christ and in the particular ministry of those who are called and ordained by Christ to serve him in the proclamation of the Gospel and in the celebration of the Sacraments. The form of this priesthood in the Church derives from the Form of Christ, the incarnate Son of God, as the Form of the Suffering Servant who came among us not to be served but to serve and give his life a ransom for many. This applies primarily to the whole Church which is baptised with Christ's own Baptism and baptised thereby into his servant-existence and ministry. But it applies also to the

institutional ministry or priesthood of those who are consecrated and set apart within the royal priesthood of the Body
of Christ, and which as such is as essential to the continuing
life and mission of the Church as Bible and Sacramental
Ordinances. Like them, and unlike the Word of God, the
institutional order of the ministry in the service of the Gospel in history will pass away at the *parousia* of the Lord Jesus
Christ, when the royal priesthood of the one Body, as distinct from the institutional priesthood, will be fully revealed.

It should be pointed out that the term 'priest' (ἱερεύς)
was never applied in the Apostolic Foundation of the Church
to the ordained ministry, but was applied only to Jesus Christ
himself and in the plural, in a corporate form, to the Church
as a whole. It was in keeping with this apostolic tradition
that priesthood was understood in classical Anglicanism.
The English word 'priest', of course, derives from '*presbyter*'
and is not a translation of '*sacerdos*', and was regularly used
in the sense of presbyter, not in the sense of a sacrificing
priest. It is particularly at the celebration of the Eucharist as
well as in the ministry of the Word, that the true nature of
the ordination to the priesthood and its Christlike functioning in the Church became apparent, for, as St Thomas
Aquinas rightly used to point out, 'ordination is in order to
the Eucharist'. This ordained ministry or priesthood is in
no sense an extension of the priestly ministry of Christ or a
prolongation of his vicarious work. That is the view that
gives rise to the very wrong notion of eucharistic sacrifice as
an extension or repetition of Christ's own priestly sacrifice,
and to wrong notions of priesthood as the prolongation of
Christ's Priesthood.

How do we offer in eucharistic worship the unique sacrifice of Christ which by its essential nature is offered by him
in our place and on our behalf and in our stead once for
all? It may be done only as our Lord commanded by way of
a *eucharistic diaconia,* that is through an offering and partak-
ing of the consecrated bread and wine as a memorial
(ἀνάμνησις) in the Name of Christ held up in prayer and
thanksgiving before God. This is an act of worship on our
part corresponding to the substitutionary nature of his activity in which he takes our place. It is not one in which as
celebrants we act in Christ's place so that we substitute for

him or displace him; rather is it one in which we serve his vicarious Priesthood, in accordance with the biblical principle 'not I but Christ' (Gal. 2.20). What we do in eucharistic thanksgiving is to hold up before God the Lord Jesus Christ in his atoning sacrifice and take refuge in his presentation of himself, and of us in him, before the Father, for he is both the one who offers and the one who is offered. This is nowhere better expressed than in William Bright's hymn:

> And now, O Father, mindful of the love,
> That bought us, once for all, on Calvary's Tree,
> And having with us him that pleads above,
> We here present, we here spread forth to thee,
> That only offering perfect in thine eyes,
> The one true, pure, immortal sacrifice.
>
> Look, Father, look on his anointed face,
> And only look on us as found in him;
> Look not on our misusings of thy grace,
> Our prayer so languid, and our faith so dim:
> For lo! between our sins and their reward,
> We set the passion of thy Son our Lord.

In the celebration of the Eucharist we give thanks and glorify the reconciling Priesthood of the one Mediator between God and man who loved us and gave himself for us. We believe that in every celebration of the Eucharist in the Name of the Father, the Son and The Holy Spirit, Christ himself, our great High Priest, is actively present and grants us so to participate in the mystery of his vicarious sacrifice that through the power of his Spirit we may really eat the flesh and drink the blood of the crucified and risen Son of Man. In a very real sense Christ Jesus is himself our worship and our eucharistic sacrifice, and it is as such that he is personally present at the Eucharist, as in the Holy Spirit we are brought into such a communion with the Father through the Son that we are given by grace to participate in the real presence of the crucified, risen and advent Lord himself.

It is strictly in accordance with this vicarious presence of Christ in the Eucharist that we must think of our part in its celebration whether as participants or as celebrants. We bring to it no status, sacrifice or worship of our own, or if we do we renounce ourselves before him and let our worship and sacrifice be displaced and replaced by the sole sufficient sacrifice of Christ. That is why we hold out empty hands at the holy table or the altar to receive the bread and the wine and partake of Christ and his sacrifice. 'Nothing in my hands I bring, simply to they cross I cling'. It is through him, with him, and in him alone, that we have access to the Father and worship him in the unity of the Holy Spirit.

In celebrating the Eucharist in this way, our priesthood is in no sense to be regarded as an extension of the priesthood of Christ. Nevertheless the diaconal form our priesthood takes in Christ, at and through the Eucharist, derives from the form of Christ as the Suffering Servant, which, as he demonstrated to his disciples at the paschal inauguration of the New Covenant in his Body and Blood, must be, not one in which they exercise authority or power, but one of self-effacing service after the pattern he himself exhibited in his coming among us not to be served but to serve.

EDINBURGH
January, 1993

I

THE ROYAL PRIEST

THE word for priest (ἱερεύς) in the New Testament derives its significance largely from the Old Testament, although the distinctive character or 'order' of priesthood reposes entirely upon the Person of Christ, our High Priest. In the Old Testament the word for priest (כֹּהֵן or כָּהַן) primarily denotes a truthsayer, or seer, i.e. one who has to do with the Word of God.[1] That is very apparent with regard to the Levitical priesthood which was concerned with the Holy Place of God's Word, the *dᵉḇîr* (דְּבִיר), as it was called. All that the priest does, all liturgical action, answers to the Word given to the priest who bears that Word and mediates it to man, and only in relation to that primary function does he have the other functions of oblation and sacrifice.

It is worth while pausing to examine the significance of the Hebrew term for word, *dāḇār* (דָּבָר).[2] This appears to derive from a Semitic root *dbr* meaning 'backside' or 'hinterground', which is apparent in the expression for the Holy of Holies just mentioned, the *dᵉḇîr*, which was lodged at the very back of the Tabernacle or Temple. The term *dāḇār* has a dual significance. On the one hand it refers to the hinterground of meaning, the inner reality of the word, but on the other hand, it refers to the dynamic event in which that inner reality becomes manifest. Thus every event has its *dāḇār* or word, so that he who understands the *dāḇār* of an event understands its real meaning.

The *Septuagint* (with some exceptions) regularly translates the Hebrew *dāḇār* either by λόγος or by ῥῆμα, while the plural *dᵉḇārîm* like the plural ῥήματα may mean 'history', like the Latin *res gestae*. It is especially in regard to the Word of God that this dual significance is apparent, particularly as the Word of God comes to the prophet and enters history as dynamic event (ὁ λόγος τοῦ κυρίου ἐγένετο). In this connexion it is also instruc-

---

[1] For the following see the article by G. Schrenk, in *Kittels Theologisches Woerterbuch zum Neuen Testament*, Bd. III, pp. 257ff.

[2] See the illuminating article by Procksch, op. cit., Bd. IV, pp. 89ff.

I

tive to find that where word and event coincide there is truth (ἀλήθεια אֱמֶת). Thus God's Word is Truth where His Action corresponds to His Word. That is characteristic of man's word too, for his word is true where there is a relation of faithfulness (אֱמוּנָה = πίστις = אֱמֶת) between the speaker and the speaking of the word, and also between the speaking of the word and the hearing of it. When such a word is credited as truth it is confirmed with 'āmēn (אָמֵן). Nowhere is that Hebraism so apparent as in the *Apocalypse* (Rev. 3.14) where Christ is spoken of as 'the Amen, the true and faithful witness' (ὁ 'Αμήν, ὁ μάρτυς ὁ πιστὸς καὶ ἀληθινός).

This is one of the dominant conceptions behind the Old Testament understanding of the cult, and indeed it looks as if the whole Tabernacle or Temple were constructed around the significance of *dāḇār*. In the very back of the Tabernacle or the Holy of Holies, the *dᵉḇîr*, there are lodged the ten Words or *dᵉḇārîm*. Those Ten Words form the innermost secret of Israel's history. It is therefore highly significant that in the Old Testament's interpretation of its own history and its ancient cult, they were lodged in the hinterground of a movable tent which formed the centre of Israel's historical pilgrimage. That Tent was called the Tent of Meeting or the Tent of Witness, for it was there that God's Word encountered Israel, and it was there that Israel kept tryst with the living and speaking God. All through Israel's history the Word enshrined in the form of *dᵉḇārîm* was hidden in the *dᵉḇîr*, but was again and again made manifest when God made bare His mighty arm and showed His glory. The coming of God's Word, the making bare of His mighty arm, and the manifestation of His glory, are all essentially cognate expressions in the Old Testament, as is apparent in the accounts of the founding and establishing of the Covenant at Mount Sinai.

The priesthood of the Old Testament is understood as functioning only within the Covenant and the saving relation with the mighty Word of God which that Covenant brought to Israel. Israel is thus made a Kingdom of Priests, a Holy People, because, as St. Paul put it, 'unto them were committed the oracles of God' (Rom. 3.2). It was within this covenant-relation so often described as 'mercy and truth' (חֶסֶד וֶאֱמֶת) that the cultus was set and that all priestly actions were carried

2

out. The whole liturgy was regarded by the Old Testament as an ordinance of grace initiated by God Himself and appointed by Him. It was not an undertaking on the part of man. It was God Himself who provided the sacrifice, and the whole action is described, therefore, in the form of a divinely appointed response to God's Word (Exod. 25.22; Num. 7.89). The sacrifices and oblations were not regarded as having any efficacy in themselves, but as having efficacy only in so far as they were liturgical obedience to the divine ordinance. They were designed to point beyond themselves to God's will to be gracious and to pardon. They were essentially *witness* and were performed within the Tabernacle of Witness or the Dwelling-Place of Testimony. All priestly action within the place of meeting was by way of acknowledgment and witness to God's testimony of Himself in the Covenant. God is not acted upon by means of priestly sacrifice. Priestly action rests upon God's Self-revelation in His Word and answers as cultic sign and action to the thing signified. That is particularly clear in regard to the teaching of the Old Testament about atonement, for the various words used to express expiation or reconciliation are used with God as Subject always, never with God as object (except in describing heathen sacrifice), and are only used with man as subject in the secondary sense of liturgical obedience to God's appointment. It is actually God Himself who performs the act of forgiveness and atonement, but the priestly cultus is designed to answer to His act and bear witness to His cleansing of the sinner.

The priesthood of the Old Testament in its double character, as mediation of God's Word and priestly witness to God's revealed Will, is given very clear interpretation in the account of the relations of Moses and Aaron, brother priests of the tribe of Levi. Moses is represented as the unique mediator, the one who talks with God face to face and mouth to mouth.[1] Because of this unique priesthood of Moses Philo called him the 'high-priestly Logos' (Kittel, op. cit., *Bd.* III, p. 259). In this supreme relation to God's Word, Moses is priest *par excellence*, whose mediatorial functions are seen as he pleads with God for Israel's forgiveness, even if it means the blotting out

---

[1] The sublime uniqueness of this can be judged from the fact that St. Paul uses the Old Testament language about Moses, Num. 12.7, to describe our knowledge not in part but in fulness when we shall know even as we are known, 1 Cor. 13.12.

3

of the name of Moses himself from before God, or as upon Horeb he intercedes for Israel in her battle with Amalek while Aaron and Hur hold up his hands in prayer. It is to Moses supremely that God reveals Himself in the establishing of the Tabernacle, and with Moses that He communes above the mercy-seat upon the Ark of Testimony (Num. 7.89; Exod. 25.22).

Over against Moses, and in secondary status, Aaron is regarded as the liturgical priest who carries out in continual cultic witness the actual mediation that came through Moses. In this way, the cult was a liturgical extension into the history of Israel and her worship of the once-and-for-all events of Exodus and Sinai. They were given permanent form in the Covenant of Law and sacrificial witness. It seems clear too that the $d^e\underline{b}\hat{i}r$, or Holy of Holies, represents cultically Mount Sinai itself as shrouded in cloud and divine glory, which Moses ascended to commune with God and to receive the divine commandments, and ascended again to intercede for Israel in her sin in fashioning and worshipping the golden calf. That which took place once and for all in the law-giving and covenantal atonement is enshrined in the liturgy of the Tabernacle. But it is extended cultically into the life and history of Israel in such a way as to make clear that the priestly sacrifices and oblations are carried out as liturgical witness to the divine glory and obedience to God's proclamation of His own Name in grace and judgment, in mercy and truth. Thus Aaron's supreme function as high priest, bearing the iniquity of the people (Exod. 28.38; Lev. 10.17; Num. 18.1, 23; cf. Lev. 16.21f; Num. 14.18f) was to ascend into the Holy of Holies once a year on the Day of Atonement. At the risk of his very life and relying upon the blood of atonement, in the strictest obedience to the divine ordinance, he was to make intercession for Israel and to receive the divine peace in a renewal of the Covenant. Then he returned from behind the veil to the waiting congregation with the blessed 'peace be unto you', to put the Name of God upon them in benediction (Num. 6.22f).

As the Old Testament came to assume its final form under the hands of the redactors this understanding of priesthood and worship was one of its main concerns. We are told of attacks upon it right from the start, of conflict between prophet and priest, between priestly mediation of the Word of God and priestly mediation in sacrificial witness, for the latter sought to make itself independent of the former. That is particularly evident in the incident of the golden calf which was the occasion of Moses' act of mediation, and of the revolt of Aaron and Miriam who challenged the uniqueness of Moses. 'Has God spoken only by Moses?' Miriam was punished by leprosy and the *S^ekînāh* or Glory of God left Aaron's Tabernacle, and once again Moses intervened in priestly intercession. On both occasions, it is shown, the continuance of the sacrificial priesthood of Aaron is dependent on the priestly mediation of Moses and on his unique relation to God.

In these two incidents we have combined the attempt to transform the Israelite cult into something more pleasurable and to make the sacrificial priesthood stand by itself, independently of the mediation of the Word. That is the story of Israel all through the centuries. The appeal of the worship of the nature gods and the feminine deities or *'Aštārôt* represents the temptation to fashion worship according to forms governed by man's desire, while the tendency to make the sacrificial priesthood independent of the prophetic Word of God represents the temptation to escape from direct meeting or encounter with the living God.[1] The more the liturgical forms ($\epsilon\tilde{\iota}\delta\eta$) are turned into idols ($\epsilon\tilde{\iota}\delta\omega\lambda\alpha$), the less men are disturbed by a speaking God. The Old Testament tells us that sin is so deeply ingrained in man that he seeks to erect the divine ordinances of worship into priestly ritual efficient in itself, and into a form that ministers to his own desires. That was certainly the great sin of Israel. She sought to make the Temple and its liturgy independent of God's Word and to assimilate it to the worship of nature, so that it became a liturgy of oblation as action upon God, as manipulation of God's will.

Against that independence and perversion of priesthood and priestly liturgy God sent the prophets, most of them out of the priesthood itself, to protest against the transmutation of liturgy into idolatry, against the transmutation of liturgical forms of witness into hardened and self-sufficient forms that only ministered to Israel's false security. The language of God's Word in the prophets is often as fierce as it is startling. 'I hate, I despise your feasts, and I will take no delight in your solemn

---

[1] Essentially the same temptations later assailed the Christian Church in the Mediterranean countries.

5

assemblies. Yea, though ye offer me your burnt offerings and meal offerings, I will not accept them: neither will I regard the peace-offerings of your fat beasts' (Amos 5.21f). Thus we have arising out of the very heart of Israelite worship a prophetic and eschatological suspension of priestly liturgy, for the answer of the day of the Lord will be darkness and not light (Amos 5.18). Instead of priestly sacrifice is demanded obedience and mercy. More and more it became the insistence of the prophets that the Word of God is dynamic action, and it is to be honoured as it is done into the flesh and blood. Unless the Word of God is done into the very existence of Israel the priestly witness of the cult is mockery. As the prophets are spurned, at last God promises to destroy the Temple and so to overthrow the false security of Israel (Jer. 7.1ff) which rested upon a sinful perversion of the divine ordinances of priesthood and worship. This perversion did not correspond to the Covenant which was sealed by circumcision in the flesh of every son of Israel, making Israel into a royal priesthood, and which demanded that the whole life of Israel within the Covenant in heart and lips and ears should answer to the revealed Will of God. True worship must be done into the flesh, and so the true worship of Israel looks forward to the day of the Lord when His Word will become event and be enacted as truth in the very heart of His people. Thus the whole intention of the cult is bent forward to point to a new Covenant when the Word of God will be inscribed upon the tables of the heart and truth will spring out of the land.

It is in line with that too that the cult-prophets, in language drawn from the priestly sacrifices, and the great salvation-events of the Exodus, liturgically extended in them, place before Israel the doctrine of the Suffering Servant. As a lamb led to the slaughter the Servant embodies in flesh and blood the Covenant of God with Israel. Here the two aspects of priesthood are brought into one, for the conceptions of Moses and Aaron are telescoped together in the vicarious life of the Servant of the Lord in order to set forth at once the redeeming action of God for Israel, and the sacrifice of obedience enacted into the life of Israel. That is the wonderful climax of the Old Testament, where it points to the union of God and man in Messianic redemption and breaks into the Gospel.

After the Exile there comes about a remarkable change in

the whole situation. We find a rehabilitation of the ancient cult in final liturgical form but we find also a rehabilitation of the Word of God, mainly in the form of 'Instruction'. Now there begins the era of liturgised law and legalised liturgy. Already the scribe emerges into prominence along with the priest. Law and liturgy go hand in hand, but in such a way that they are made self-sufficient and independent, liturgised Scripture and legalised priestcraft. Here there is no room for the prophet, the direct intervention of the charismatic Word, for the Word of God is made of none effect by the traditions of men. In this developing situation Ezekiel had already seen the *S͘ekînāh* leaving the Temple as it had left Aaron's Tabernacle in his revolt from Moses, and the seventy-fourth Psalm says: 'We see not our signs. There is no more any prophet.' Without the priestly mediation of the Word of God and its dynamic intervention in the life of Israel, Israel is delivered over to God-forsakenness, hardened by sin in the very use of the ordinances of grace. And Daniel speaks of the sealing up of sins and the sealing up of vision and prophecy until the coming of the Anointed (ch. 9.24f).

That is the situation into which Jesus Christ was born: at last the Word of God, who cast His shadow over the cult of Israel and came to the prophets, was made flesh and tabernacled among men, full of grace and truth (John 1.14f). The *S͘ekînāh* glory of God dwells in a Man. He is Himself both the Lamb of God and the Temple of God (John 1.29-36; 4.21f). But the coming of the Word of God back among His own, where it had not been received, means the breaking in of the Kingdom of God into the sphere of liturgised Scripture and legalised liturgy, into the bondage of scribe and priest (John 1.19f). The Day of the Lord so long desired is a day of judgment, but also of new life. 'Destroy this temple, and in three days I will raise it up' (John 2.19). Here where the Word of the living God is made flesh, the two aspects of priesthood are combined and fulfilled. Jesus Christ comprised in Himself both God's saving action toward man, and man's perfect obedience toward God (John 5.17-47). He is Himself (*Ἐγώ Εἰμι*—John 6.35; 8.12; 10.7; 10.11; 11.25; 14.6; 15.1), the complete form of the divine action, the Word made flesh, and the perfect form of the human response in obedience to the Father. 'I and my Father are one' (John 10.30). Therefore He can say, 'I am the way, the truth, and the life. No man cometh unto the Father but by me' (John 14.6).

That is what we see in the pages of the Synoptic Gospels. Jesus steps into the tradition of the cult-prophets and it is primarily as Word of God that He approaches the Cross, but it is the Word made flesh. He is at once the Word of God to man and for the first time a real word of man to God.[1] As true God and true Man, in hypostatic union in one Person, He steps into the tension between the covenant faithfulness of God and the unfaithfulness of man in order to realise within man's enmity to God the complete oneness of God and man. In Jesus Christ, the Word tabernacling among men, we have the ultimate and final meeting of God and man to which the Tent of Meeting in the Old Testament pointed forward. But here we have the complete Word of God to man in grace and truth, and the complete witness of man to God's grace and truth, in one. Here we have One who steps into the midst of our religious estrangement from God which rests upon a perversion both of Scripture and priesthood, and calls scribe and priest alike to account. He is the Word who has power on earth to forgive sins and to cleanse the sick. He has authority over the Sabbath and over the Temple itself, which He insists on cleansing before the 'hour' of sacrifice. He is the Messiah, the Anointed One, Prophet, Priest, and King in One, the Lord Himself suddenly come to His Temple. Throughout, it is primarily as Word of God that Christ presses toward reconciliation, and insists that in His Word God's own sovereign Kingdom breaks in.

That means that Jesus insists on the subordination of priesthood and priestly function to God's sovereign initiative and royal grace. And so, first of all, He steps into the place of the Prophet, and as the Word made flesh proclaims the Word of forgiveness and healing and peace, and only then in priestly obedience to the Word of God does He advance to the living and actual liturgy of atonement. The primacy of the Word of forgiveness and cleansing is seen in the fact that Jesus does not speak of Himself in cultic terms, nor does He draw upon liturgical imagery in His parables, and only very occasionally in His teaching. It is seen also in the instance when after forgiveness and healing He sends a man back to the priests

[1] Cf. Heb. 4.12f: ζῶν ὁ λόγος τοῦ θεοῦ ... πρὸς ὃν ἡμῖν ὁ λόγος.

8

(Matt. 8.4; Mark 14.4; Luke 5.14), for a witness to them (εἰς μαρτύριον αὐτοῖς), so that the priests with the appropriate sacrifices may bear witness to the sovereign action of the Word spoken by Christ in cleansing and healing. That is to say, Jesus forces the priesthood into its proper function of witness to the Truth, of liturgical acknowledgment of what God has done and spoken in His grace. The significant fact is that, while in Word Jesus exercises His prophetic ministry, in His action He exercises His priestly ministry. It is as Suffering Servant of the Lord that He combines both.

It is that combination that comes out so strongly in the Fourth Gospel. The very Prologue, as we have seen, begins with the Word that was hid in the bosom of the Father, but now comes forth into history (ὁ λόγος ἐγένετο), tabernacling among men after the pattern of the dāḇār of the Old Testament cult. And witness is born to His manifest glory, full of grace and truth. It is particularly the liturgy of the Day of Atonement with its ascent into the Holy of Holies that is to be discerned transmuted in the Gospel story. From the beginning we have combined the thought of the 'Isaianic' Lamb led to the slaughter as Suffering Servant with the 'Pentateuchal' Lamb which, as well as the officiating priest, is washed at the laver, before sacrifice on the altar takes place. And so the ancient priestly liturgy enacted in the flesh is pressed through the cleansing of the Temple, through the feasts of the year, to the last week which gathers up and recapitulates the whole cultic action, when we see Christ with high-priestly intercession offering Himself in sacrifice as the Lamb of God. He is at once Victim and Priest, at once the Judged and the Intercessor. Then after ascending to the throne of the Father the risen Christ returns to His waiting people with the liturgical 'Peace be unto you' of reconciliation with God, and enacts the blessing by breathing upon them the Holy Spirit (John 20.17 ff).

When we turn to the Epistles of the New Testament for the theology of Christ's priestly ministry, we find two main emphases which very clearly correspond to the two main aspects of priesthood adumbrated in the Old Testament and fulfilled so wonderfully in Christ Himself: the mediation of God's Word, and liturgical witness to it, and overarching both, as in the Gospels, the concept of the Messianic Kingdom. This

9

dual aspect is most evident in the Epistles of St. Paul, on the one hand, which are concerned mainly with atonement in terms of justification and expiation before the Word or Law of God, and in the Epistle to the Hebrews, on the other hand, which is most concerned with atonement in terms of Christ's high-priestly oblation of Himself and His heavenly Intercession. The difference between these two, however, is not one of contrariety but of emphasis. They imply each other and they are correlative to each other. A New Testament doctrine of the Priesthood of Christ and His sacrifice rests upon that twin foundation. The Epistle to the Hebrews is addressed to those concerned with the Jewish liturgy, and speaks in terms of those Old Testament actions whose clear fulfilment is seen in Christ, such as the relation of Christ's ascension to the ascension of the high priest into the Holy of Holies, but here very little is said about the resurrection or the forty days on earth of Christ, as there is no analogy to that in the Old Testament cultus. St. Paul, on the other hand, concentrates a good deal of attention on the resurrection of Christ and the significance which it casts upon the act of atonement on the Cross. He uses priestly language from the Old Testament only at crucial points in his doctrine of atonement and thinks primarily of God's ordinance of grace, and of the revelation of His righteousness. It is when St. Paul comes to expound the Christian life and ministry in their witness to the death of Christ that he employs the priestly language of sacrifice. Liturgy for St. Paul is primarily the liturgy of life in flesh and blood as witness to the death and resurrection. In this way the liturgy of the Lord's Supper is acted out in the life of the One Body which bears about the dying of the Lord Jesus that the life also of Christ might be made manifest in our mortal bodies. In other words, the λογικὴ λατρεία or the λειτουργία is the Eucharistic life of the new humanity which the Church is given in Jesus Christ and which it fulfils as His Body. Thus it is mainly to St. Paul that we turn for our understanding of the priesthood of the Church (ἱερατεία, ἱεράτευμα), and mainly to the Author of the Epistle to the Hebrews that we turn for our understanding of the High Priesthood of Christ.

It will be sufficient here to focus our attention upon one significant passage, Hebrews 3.1ff, 'Wherefore, holy brethren, partakers of the heavenly calling (κλήσεως ἐπουρανίου μέτοχοι) consider the Apostle and High Priest of our profession, Jesus (κατανοήσατε τὸν Ἀπόστολον καὶ Ἀρχιερέα τῆς ὁμολογίας ἡμῶν Ἰησοῦν), who was faithful to him that appointed him (πιστὸν ὄντα τῷ ποιήσαντι αὐτόν), as was Moses in all his house (ὡς καὶ Μωϋσῆς ἐν ὅλῳ τῷ οἴκῳ αὐτοῦ).' Here we have described Christ's twofold function in priestly mediation. He is the Apostle or *Sālîaḥ* of God,[1] and He is also our High Priest made in all points as we are, but without sin. This double ministry is of God's making or appointment, and in this double ministry Christ remains utterly faithful (πιστόν).

The writer has already explained that Christ is God's Son, His full and final revelation. He is the Word or Son of the Father sent into the world, and is therefore God's Apostle. This is the primary emphasis in the Epistle, and only after stating that the Apostle moves on to speak of Christ as High Priest, but in such a way as to make it clear that His High Priesthood is part of His Sonship, and has no independent status or function (cf. 5.5f). As such Jesus perfectly fulfils and far transcends all that Moses represented in the Old Testament. And so he goes on to say: 'Moses verily was faithful in all his house, as a servant (Num. 12.7) for a testimony of those things which were to be spoken after (καὶ Μωϋσῆς μὲν πιστὸς ἐν ὅλῳ τῷ οἴκῳ αὐτοῦ ὡς θεράπων εἰς μαρτύριον τῶν λαληθησομένων); but Christ as a Son over his own house (Χριστὸς δὲ ὡς υἱὸς ἐπὶ τὸν οἶκον αὐτοῦ), whose house are we, if we hold fast the confidence and rejoicing of the hope firm unto the end.'

The concept that lies behind this is that of the 'son of the house'. The Hebrew for that, בֶּן־בַּיִת, is variously translated in the *Septuagint*. Sometimes it is rendered by οἰκονόμος or householder, in the sense of οἰκοδεσπότης (= אֲשֶׁר צַל הַבַּיִת). But οἰκονόμος can also be used of the slave or the chief steward in a household. In this sense it is applied to Moses, as in the passage from Numbers 12.7 referred to above. Moses is the בֶּן־בַּיִת or οἰκονόμος in God's House and Aaron is subordinate to him. But when the term οἰκονόμος is applied to a servant it is also rendered by the term δοῦλος, and both are used of Moses.

In the New Testament we find all three Greek terms being used for the Hebrew בֶּן־בַּיִת. In the parables of Jesus οἰκονόμος and δοῦλος both describe the 'son of the house' (cf.

Luke 12.42f and Matt. 24.45f), or the faithful steward (πιστὸς οἰκονόμος) or faithful servant (πιστὸς δοῦλος). It is the same Hebrew term behind this passage in Hebrews 3, but here the בֵּן בַּיִת is interpreted as δοῦλος when it refers to Moses and as υἱός when it refers to Christ. Moses is faithful *in* all his house as a servant (θεράπων being used to make very clear His relation to Christ[1]), and compared to Christ his ministry is described in terms of witness (εἰς μαρτύριον τῶν λαληθησομένων), Christ is the real בֵּן בַּיִת who exercises His ministry as the consecrated Son (Heb. 7.28) *over* His house, whose house we are, i.e. the Church.

In this particular passage the work of Christ as Apostle and High Priest, both in the sense of 'the Son over the House,' is described in terms of confession, ὁμολογία, a word which comes in three other passages (3.1; 4.14; 10.23). In each case it sets forth primarily the confession made by the High Priest as he enters within the veil. It is the confession of our sin before God and the confession of God's righteous judgment upon our sin. As Apostle Christ bears witness for God, that He is Holy. As High Priest He acknowledges that witness and says Amen to it. Again as Apostle of God He confesses the mercy and grace of God, His will to pardon and reconcile. As High Priest He intercedes for men, and confesses them before the face of God. But this confession and intercession are not to be understood in terms of word only, but in terms of the actual historical events of the life and passion of Christ. And so the Epistle to the Hebrews speaks of that in terms of the actual life and obedience of Jesus in which, as Apostle of God and High Priest, He carried through His relations with sinners to the end, to the completion of His work on the Cross, thus becoming the Author and Perfecter of our faith.

That is just what we see in the account of the Gospels. As God and yet as Man Christ steps into our midst to overcome our estrangement and to reconcile us to the Father. From the side of God He acts in the steadfastness of divine truth and love in judgment, from the side of man He acts in unswerving obedience to the Father. In that unity of the divine-human steadfastness the Word of God is spoken, the Word of Truth and Grace is enacted in our existence of flesh and blood, and

---

[1] On the Day of Atonement the high priest was regarded as Šáliah of God not of men. See W. Manson, *The Epistle to the Hebrews*, p. 54.

the answer of man is given in the obedience of a perfect life, in the prayer which is the whole assent of Jesus to the will of God as it confronts the will of man: 'Not my will but thine be done.' That is the prayer which He teaches His people and puts on their lips: 'Our Father which art in Heaven, hallowed be thy name, thy kingdom come, thy will be done on earth as it is in heaven.'

In this unity of truth and faithfulness from the side of God and from the side of man, Jesus endured the Cross. There He witnessed a good confession before Pontius Pilate, in which the Early Church saw an earthly counterpart to His confession before the Heavenly Father, to which those other words refer: 'Him that confesses me before men, I will confess before my Father in heaven.' But this confession of Christ as Apostle and as High Priest is not in word only, for at the Cross it becomes the actual judgment of God, and the actual submission of Christ in perfect obedience to the point of death. It is actualised confession once and for all in historical event. It is this very actualisation as event, the fulfilled liturgy of Word and Oblation, which takes the sacrifice of Jesus out of the sphere of mere cult or liturgical action, and tells us that liturgical action is only witness to concrete reality. But while this is concrete historical reality, it is also eternal spiritual reality, for Christ has opened up through His atonement a new and living way to the Father. After His ascension He ever lives before the face of the Father as our *Leitourgos* and Intercessor, for there He confesses us before the face of God as those for whom He died, as those whose names He has entered as members of His Body.

Because that is Christ's confession, it is also our confession. We may now take His confession as our own, His answer of prayer on our lips, and in His Name go boldly before the throne of grace. That confession is the one thing we hold on to. It is the confession of our hope, for all our hope rests on the obedience of Christ on the Cross and His confession before the Father. The confession of the Church which answers to the confession of the High Priest is the sacrifice of praise and thanksgiving to God continually. The reconciliation wrought by Christ has been completed once and for all and by its very nature cannot be repeated, but it is given a counterpart in the Church in the form of Eucharistic prayer and praise.

13

There are three facts of cardinal importance here which must be stressed.

(a) In Jesus Christ, as Apostle and High Priest, both aspects of priesthood are fulfilled, but they are fulfilled in His Sonship and on the ground of His Sonship. He is not priest in the sense that He symbolises, or bears priestly witness to, something else, what God does. No, He is the Son of God, God Himself come down as Priest to share our humanity. On the ground of His Sonship and His incarnational qualification He ascends into the Holies. Here we pass beyond the conception of Aaronic priesthood to priesthood of another order. He is Priest in final reality, fulfilling the Mosaic priesthood because His Word is identical with Kingly act; fulfilling the Aaronic priesthood because His offering is identical with His Person. This is Royal Priesthood, in the coincidence of Grace and Omnipotence, in the identity of Person and Work. As such it is as unique as God Himself.

(b) Both parts of priesthood are fulfilled *for us*. The act of God in Christ for us, and the act of man in Christ for us, are inseparable, in an atonement of substitutionary nature. It is not only that as Son of God, or Apostle from God, Christ has done for us what we could not do, but that as High Priest in our humanity He has done for us what we could not do. He has once and for all offered to God our obedience, our response, our witness, our amen. He became our brother man and He offered on our behalf a human obedience, a human response, a human witness and a human amen, so that in Him our human answer to God in life, worship, and prayer is already completed. He is in the fullest sense our ὁμολογία. It can only be ours, therefore, if it involves the setting aside (ἀθέτησις) of the obedience, response, witness, amen, and even the worship and prayer which we offer on our own. The radical significance of Christ's substitutionary Priesthood does not lie in the fact that His perfect Self-offering perfects and completes our imperfect offerings, but that these are displaced by His completed Self-offering. We can only offer what has already been offered on our behalf, and offer it by the only mode appropriate to such a substitutionary offering, by prayer, thanksgiving and praise.

(c) Christ Jesus who offered Himself to God for us through the Eternal Spirit has ascended and ever lives as our Intercessor. It is as our Brother, wearing our humanity, that He

14

has ascended, presenting Himself eternally before the face of the Father, and presenting us in Himself. As such He is not only our word to God but God's Word to us. Toward God He is our Advocate and High Priest, but toward man He is the assurance of the divine peace and love toward us, of God's acceptance of us in Himself. The very Spirit through whom He offered Himself eternally to the Father He has sent down upon us in His high-priestly blessing, fulfilling in the life of His Church on earth that which He has fulfilled on our behalf in the heavenlies. That is the indescribable mystery which the *Apocalypse* seeks to put into words in its opening chapter: the presence through the Spirit of the risen Christ in the midst of His Church on earth. 'Clothed with a garment down to the foot and girt about the paps with a golden girdle', He is the Royal High Priest. 'Unto him that loved us and washed us from our sins in his own blood, and made us kings and priests unto God; to him be glory and dominion for ever and ever. Amen.' (Rev. 1.5f).

The Epistle to the Hebrews speaks of this Royal Priesthood of Christ, 'the consecrated Son', in the following terms: 'We have such an high priest who is set on the right hand of the throne of the majesty in the heavens, a minister ($\Lambda\epsilon\iota\tau\sigma\nu\rho\gamma\acute{o}s$) of the sanctuary, and of the true tabernacle, which the Lord pitched and not man. For every high priest is ordained to offer gifts and sacrifices: wherefore it is of necessity that this man have somewhat also to offer' (Heb. 7.28; 8.1-3). The word *Leitourgos* used here very fittingly describes the Royal Priest, as an examination of its Biblical use makes clear.

In profane Greek the words $\lambda\epsilon\iota\tau\sigma\nu\rho\gamma\epsilon\hat{\iota}\nu$ and $\lambda\epsilon\iota\tau\sigma\nu\rho\gamma\acute{\iota}a$ have a political and corporate sense. They refer to the work, $\acute{\epsilon}\rho\gamma\sigma\nu$, of the $\lambda a\acute{o}s$, i.e. they refer to the people's work or the people's service conceived in terms of corporate public duty. But that is gathered up to a head and is representatively undertaken by the chief of state or the king, who can therefore be spoken of as $\lambda\epsilon\iota\tau\sigma\nu\rho\gamma\grave{o}s$ and as exercising $\lambda\epsilon\iota\tau\sigma\nu\rho\gamma\acute{\iota}a$, both in the cultic and civil sense. That corporate and kingly connotation fits in very well with the Biblical notion of royal priesthood, though there is no Hebrew word or expression to correspond properly to the Greek significance of $\lambda\epsilon\iota\tau\sigma\nu\rho\gamma\epsilon\hat{\iota}\nu$ and its cognates.

In the Septuagint this term is never used of civil or of profane service, but only of cultic service (cf. Ezek. 44.12; 2 Chron. 18.16) and that is the sense in which it is employed in the New Testament (cf. Heb. 9.21; 10.11; 8.2, 6; Luke 1.23). In this sense the word λειτουργεῖν often translates the Hebrew שָׁרֵת, which means to serve, attend, wait on. When שָׁרֵת is used generally it is translated by δουλεύειν, but when it is used cultically it is generally rendered by λειτουργεῖν, and sometimes by λατρεύειν, διακονεῖν, δουλεύειν, θεραπεύειν. On the other hand, the noun λειτουργία, in the Septuagint, generally renders עֲבֹדָה, service, when it is used cultically and when the notion of servant-ministry is predominant. In other words, it is used of priestly service in the liturgy of Tabernacle or Temple. Once (Dan. 7.10) it is used also of angelic adoration of God, and is used frequently in the Book of Wisdom of prayer and adoration.

Thus the words λειτουργεῖν and λειτουργία in the Greek Old Testament are used almost exclusively of the sacrificial cultus. But in the New Testament there is a decided change (διόρθωσις —Heb. 9.8). As Christian terms they are used with priestly and even sacrificial *nuance*, but they are no longer used of ceremonies or religious observances. They are used of the ministry of the whole Church *vis-à-vis* the heavenly ministry of Christ. And so Christ is spoken of as the *Leitourgos* of the heavenly worship in the Tabernacle of Truth, which the Lord pitched and not man (Heb. 8.2). Surrounding Him as a flame of fire are His ministers or *leitourgoi* (Heb. 1.7), the liturgical spirits (λειτουργικὰ πνεύματα) sent forth in ministry (εἰς διακονίαν ἀποστελλόμενα) to those who shall be the heirs of salvation (Heb. 1.14).

On the other hand, the terms λειτουργεῖν and λειτουργία are used as a rule in the New Testament of the life and work of the Church and its ministry, in prayer and the preaching of the Gospel. Thus in Acts 13.2 λειτουργεῖν is used of prayer in connexion with ordination to missionary activity, and Paul, one of those thus ordained by the laying on of hands, can speak of himself as Christ's *leitourgos* to the Gentiles, describing his missionary activity as ἱερουργεῖν τὸ εὐαγγέλιον (Rom. 15.16). At the same time Paul can speak of the service of love as 'a liturgy of thanksgiving to God' (2 Cor. 9.12). In the same way he uses the verb λειτουργεῖν to speak of the ministry of Gentiles

16

to the mother church in Jerusalem, in carnal things, in monetary support (Rom. 15.27),[1] or of the service of the Philippian church through Epaphroditus to himself, ministering to his need (Phil. 2.25f). Then there is the astonishing passage in Phil. 2.17 where Paul speaks of his approaching martyrdom as a sacrificial libation 'offered upon the sacrifice and service of your faith' (ἐπὶ τῇ θυσίᾳ καὶ λειτουργίᾳ τῆς πίστεως ὑμῶν).

In all these passages Paul directs liturgical action to the life and work of the Church spending itself in the Gospel, and in Christian ministry of love of one to another. This liturgy of life and love in the Gospel he sees as the embodied liturgy of thanksgiving to God. This is liturgy done into the flesh, enacted in the body, as sacrificial oblation to God, θυσία, προσφορὰ and εὐωδία (2 Cor. 2.15; Eph. 5.2; Rom. 12.16; 15.16; Phil. 2.17; 4.18; Acts 24.17).

This brings us back to the word θυσία, which Hebrews 8.3 used to speak of the sacrifice of the Royal Priest. In the Greek Bible this word is used regularly for the Hebrew זֶבַח and מִנְחָה, referring to substitutionary sacrifice which is to be realised in life. Similarly in the New Testament it is used of an offering due and appropriate to God; but which is realised in the life and fellowship of the Church (Rom. 12.1; Phil. 2.17; 4.18; Heb. 13.15, 16; 1 Pet. 2.5; Heb. 10.5-8). Christ was once and for all sacrificed in our stead on the Cross but He has ascended into the Holy Place and ever lives to present Himself (and us *in Him* because of Himself *for us*) before the face of the Father. That sacrificial act of Christ once and for all performed and enduring in His endless life in the presence of God, is realised in the life of His people, not by repetition of His substitutionary sacrifice, but by their dying and rising with Christ in faith and life, and by the worship of self-presentation to God (Rom. 12.1; 1 Pet. 2.5). This sacrifice of the Church in worship, ministry, and life is entirely non-propitiatory, non-piacular. It is essentially eucharistic. 'Ye also, as lively stones are built up a spiritual house, an holy priesthood (οἰκοδομεῖσθε

---

[1] In line with this Paul's visit to the Church in Jerusalem is described by the word ἀναβαίνειν (Acts 18.22), which is the regular word used for the ascent to Jerusalem to the Temple, and the ascent within the Temple into the Holy of Holies. The Hebrew equivalent is עָלָה, and the corresponding noun also means oblation, עֹלָה. As such it was also applied to the ascension of Christ, speaking of His ascent into the Holy Place, and of His Self-oblation.

οἶκος πνευματικὸς εἰς ἱεράτευμα ἅγιον), to offer up spiritual
sacrifices, acceptable to God by Jesus Christ. Ye are a chosen
generation, a royal priesthood (βασίλειον ἱεράτευμα), an holy
nation, a peculiar people; that ye should shew forth the praise
of him who hath called you out of darkness into his marvellous
light' (1 Pet. 2.5, 10; cf. Exod. 19.16; Isa. 61.6).

What are meant here by 'spiritual sacrifices' (πνευματικαὶ
θυσίαι)? This expression is closely related to St. Paul's 'rational
worship' (λογικὴ λατρεία, Rom. 12.1). It may help us to
appreciate the significance of that by recalling another element
in the teaching of the Old Testament. 'And now, O Israel, what
doth the Lord thy God require of thee, but to fear the Lord
thy God, to walk in all his ways, and to love him, and to serve
the Lord thy God with all thy heart and with all thy soul'
(λατρεύειν κυρίῳ τῷ θεῷ σοῦ ἐξ ὅλης τῆς καρδίας σοῦ καὶ ἐξ
ὅλης τῆς ψυχῆς σοῦ, Deut. 10.12f; cf. Deut. 11.1). In the
Septuagint the word λατρεύειν used here may be an equivalent
for θύειν, 'to sacrifice to the Lord' (Exod. 8.4, 16), while the
noun, λατρεία, is used generally of Israel's worship at the
Passover (Exod. 12.25f; 13.5). In some respects it is more or
less equivalent to λειτουργία, and translates the same Hebrew
word (עֲבֹדָה). As such it is found also in the New Testament
(Heb. 9.6; 10.2).

The worship of God in heart and mind remains, however,
the distinctive characteristic of λατρεία. In that sense the
supreme type of sacrifice was the thank-offering, or the sacrifice of praise (Lev. 7.11f; Heb. 13.15; 1 Pet. 2.9). Thus 'the
Rabbis declare that, in the Messianic Era, all sacrifices will be
unnecessary except the thank-offering. All sacrifices shall have
completed their educational mission—all save the one incul-
cating the duty of gratitude. That sacrifice is to continue for
ever.'[1]

It was worship in that Messianic and eschatological sense
that the word λατρεία came to denote. That is apparent right
away on the pages of the New Testament. Zechariah, the
father of John the Baptist, recalls the Messianic promises spoken
by the mouth of the prophets: 'That he would grant unto us,
that we being delivered out of the hand of our enemies might
serve him without fear, in holiness and righteousness (λατρεύειν
αὐτῷ ἐν ὁσιότητι καὶ δικαιοσύνῃ) before him all the days of our

[1] J. H. Hertz, The Pentateuch and Haftorahs, Leviticus, p. 60.

life' (Luke 1.74). Thus the New Testament regards the Old Testament worship as pointing beyond itself to a Messianic fulfilment in the Kingdom of God (Luke 2.37f; Acts 26.7).

This eschatological change is very clearly brought out in the Epistle to the Hebrews (12.28). The Holy Spirit signifies by the very nature of the liturgical ordinances of the Old Testament their imperfection (Heb. 9.8). Those ordinances were carnal waiting for the time of reformation (μέχρι καιροῦ διορθώσεως, Heb. 9.10) which was fulfilled with the coming of Christ. 'How much more shall the blood of Christ who through the eternal Spirit offered himself without spot to God, purge your conscience from dead works to serve the living God?' (Heb. 9.14). That contrast between the *latreia* of the Old Testament and the *latreia* of the New Testament is wonderfully worked out in the twelfth and thirteenth chapters of the Epistle. Here we have a new understanding of worship in terms of the finished work of Christ and in terms of the Spirit, in which we are free to worship God in true fear and love, in new obedience to the new commandment of love.

There are two predominant ideas here. (*a*) The sacrifice of Christ has cleansed our conscience from fear and anxiety for legal justification, and we live in thankfulness. (*b*) The Spirit has liberated us from the dead works and carnal ordinances of ritual, so that here worship concerns the life of the whole people. It is the living worship of the whole body (cf. also Acts 24.14; 2 Tim. 1.3; Phil. 3.3; Rom. 1.9). *Latreia* is worship of God in Spirit and Truth (John 4.22f).

This 'spiritual worship', however, does not mean worship without any ordinances, for our *bodies* as well as our *hearts* are involved in this worship. 'Let us draw near with a true heart in full assurance of faith, having our *hearts* sprinkled from an evil conscience and our *bodies* washed with pure water' (Heb. 10.22). The great characteristic of this *latreia* is that it envisages a relation between the worship on earth and in body to worship in the heavenly realm.

There is a parallel here between the worship in the Old Testament Church and in the New Testament Church. The worship of God in the Tabernacle was related to a heavenly pattern (ὑπόδειγμα) shown to Moses on Mount Sinai (Heb. 8.5, 9.23f; Exod. 25.9, 40; 26.30; 27.8). Christian worship is regarded as having a similar relation to the heavenly realm.

'Ye are come unto mount Sion, and unto the city of the living God, the heavenly Jerusalem, and to an innumerable company of angels, to the general assembly and church of the first-born which are written in heaven, and to God the Judge of all and to the spirits of just men made perfect, and to Jesus the mediator of the new covenant, and to the blood of sprinkling that speaks better things than that of Abel . . . Wherefore we receiving a kingdom which cannot be moved, let us have grace whereby we may serve God (λατρεύωμεν τῷ θεῷ) accept-ably with reverence and godly fear: for our God is a consuming fire' (Heb. 12.22-24, 28, 29).

How are we to think of the relation between the *latreia* on earth and the *latreia* in Heaven?

The Epistle to the Hebrews regards the Old Testament *latreia* as a *parable* (Heb. 9.9), as a *shadow* (Heb. 8.5; 10.1), as a *type* (Heb. 8.5; 9.24) of the heavenly reality, and in that sense a ὑπόδειγμα (Heb. 8.5; 9.23f): a shadowy representation put forward in carnal commandments signifying a higher reality. When Christ came in Body and the full reality was manifest, the old patterns of worship were taken away and completely set aside (Heb. 7.18; cf. 9.26). But now that Christ has ascended and entered within the veil into the Holy Place, and intercedes for us as our *Leitourgos* in the Tabernacle of Truth, how are we to regard our Christian worship as a ὑπόδειγμα of the heavenly liturgy?

Unfortunately the Old Testament notion of the Tabernacle liturgy as in some sense signifying a heavenly pattern was given interpretation by Jewish circles in Alexandria in terms of the Platonic doctrine of imitation (μίμησις). Thus the worship on earth is not only a shadowy manifestation of the heavenly worship but in some sense a transcription of it.

That is precisely what the Epistle to the Hebrews avoids. The word for pattern in the Old Testament תַּבְנִית is translated in the Septuagint either by παράδειγμα or by εἶδος, two important terms used in the Platonic philosophy to express the eternal forms or the exemplars of the eternal forms. It is highly signi-ficant that the Epistle to the Hebrews will not use those terms, and takes the liberty of correcting the Septuagint by using instead an obscure word, ὑπόδειγμα (found in Ezek. 42.15). By that is meant that the worship on earth is not a transcrip-tion of the heavenly reality, but a pointer in observable form to a higher reality. And in order to make very sure that the ὑπόδειγμα is not to be regarded in any eternal or Platonic sense, he points out that it requires the cleansing blood of atonement (Heb. 9.22ff). It was an imperfect ὑπόδειγμα and would in due course pass away. It was only a shadow cast ahead by the coming reality and had no efficacy in itself. Its efficacy lay in liturgical obedience to what God had done and was to do.

It is in that way too that we are to think of the relation between the worship of the Christian Church on earth and the heavenly worship. Even this heavenly worship comes under the Blood of Christ, so that the *latreia* of the Church triumphant as well as the Church militant comes under the cleansing of Christ (cf. Col. 1.20). The *latreia* of the New Testament is rather different from the *latreia* of the Old Testament, because here we have the reality of Christ through the Spirit, so that the forms of worship come under judgment by that reality. What is supremely important is obedience to Christ who takes our place and whose sacrifice once and for all displaces us and relativises all cosmic forms of worship (cf. ἅγιον κοσμικόν, Heb. 9.1).

How, then, in Christian worship are we to understand ὑπόδειγμα? In answer we can only turn to the historical Christ and observe the pattern which He gives us, for it is He, our High Priest, who has entered within the veil and is our *Leitour-gos*, who supplies us with a concrete ὑπόδειγμα. It is above all to the Upper Room that we turn where Jesus celebrated the Last Supper, and where He showed us in action how we may *serve Him*. 'Ye call me Master and Lord, and ye say well; for so I am. If I then your Lord and Master have washed your feet; ye also ought to wash one another's feet. For I have given unto you a ὑπόδειγμα, that ye should do as I have done unto you. Verily, verily I say unto you, the servant is not greater than his Lord, neither he that is sent greater than he that sent him' (John 13.13f).[1] The pattern for the Church's worship and its relation to the heavenly worship is to be discerned in the Suffering Servant (cf. Jas. 5.10). The way in which the Church draws near to God is the way of the Son of Man.

In gathering up this discussion, we may observe that while

---

[1] cf. the use of ὑπογραμμός in 1 Pet. 2.21.

the New Testament uses priestly language to speak of the Royal Priesthood of Christ in His Word and Action, it also applies priestly language to the Church, showing that the Church is given to participate in His ministry, in word, deed, and life; in word, by proclaiming the Gospel to the nations, by prayer and worship and praise and thanksgiving; in life and deed, by self-sacrifice, by ministering humbly to the needs of others, and by presenting our bodies in worship to God. In this unity of word and deed, of worship and mission, in the life of the Church as the Israel of God under the rubric of the Suffering Servant, we have the fulfilment of what the cult-prophets of the Old Testament saw from afar. Whenever the priestly cult was divorced from the whole life and body of Israel, they withstood it in the name of the Lord. The Word must be done into the flesh, the priestly liturgy must be enacted in life and obedience. Within that actualisation, described as circumcision of the heart or penitence, the cult has its proper place, as Psalm 51 makes so clear. Otherwise it is only what the Epistle to the Hebrews calls a 'carnal commandment' (Heb. 7.16). Likewise the Christian liturgy, the Church's priestly ministry, divorced from the life of the whole Body, is 'of the flesh'. Christian liturgy and priesthood have their place within baptismal incorporation of the Church into the Body of Christ. The pattern of that liturgy and priesthood derives from the Suffering Servant and is to be enacted in the Body. That is our rational worship.

What does the New Testament mean by the Body?

II

THE FUNCTION OF THE BODY OF CHRIST

WE cannot pay too much attention to the fact that the Holy Spirit was sent upon the Church after the crucifixion, resurrection, and the ascension of Christ. In that series Pentecost belongs as one of the mighty salvation events, and to that series the *parousia* will belong as the last. The Church has its existence and mission between the penultimate event and the ultimate event, that is, in 'the last times' that are fully inaugurated by the descent of the Spirit (Acts 2.17), for it is through the Creator Spirit that the saving work of Christ is actualised in the Church as redemption (ἀπολύτρωσις, Eph. 1.7, 14; 4.30) reaching out to the *parousia*, demanding and pressing toward the redemption of the body (σῶμα, Romans 8.23), and indeed the whole creation.

When we ask the New Testament how that operates, we are given a threefold answer.

(*a*) The Spirit operates by creating out of the world a body (σῶμα) which St. Paul calls the Body of Christ.[1] The Creator Spirit is God in His freedom to be present to the creature and to realise the relation of the creature to Himself in being and in life.[2] But here on the ground of the reconciling work of Christ the Spirit forms out of our humanity a body where the old creation is opened up from within for the reception and actualisation of revelation and reconciliation. As such this body becomes matched to Christ as His *vis-à-vis* in history[3] and as the instrument of His saving purpose in the Gospel. It is the sphere where through the presence of the Spirit the salvation-events of the birth, life, death, resurrection and ascension are operative here and now within history, the sphere where within the old creation the new creation has broken in with power.

---

[1] Our whole discussion of this subject today has been greatly helped by J. A. T. Robinson in his superb book, *The Body*.

[2] See K. Barth, *The Doctrine of the Word of God*, p. 515f.

[3] Cf. 1 Cor. 6.13: 'The body is for the Lord and the Lord for the body' (τὸ δὲ σῶμα τῷ κυρίῳ, καὶ ὁ κύριος τῷ σώματι).

(*b*) This body (σῶμα) reaches out through the Spirit to fulfilment (πλήρωμα) in a movement which takes place intensively within the body as it is rooted and grounded in love and grows up into the fulness of Christ (Eph. 3.17; 4.13, etc.), but which takes place extensively as well, reaching out both to the ends of the earth and to the ends of the ages (Eph. 1.23; 4.10, etc.). It is at once a teleological and an eschatological movement of fulfilment.

(*c*) This movement takes place through operation of Word and Sacraments. With the descent of the Spirit in power from on High the witness of the Church to the death and resurrection of Christ takes the field as *kerygma*, i.e. such preaching that the Lord works with the Church confirming the Word with signs following (Mark 16.20). It is thus as Word of God that it grows, increases, gathers strength, and is multiplied (Acts 6.7; 12.24; 19.20), and all who believe and are baptised into the name of Christ are added by God to the Body (Acts 2.41, 47; 5.14; 11.24).

In the whole relation of Spirit and Body we have to remember the inseparable relation in the Bible between רוּחַ and דָּבָר, πνεῦμα and λόγος, where the basic conception is of the living Breath of God uttering His Word, so that reception of the Spirit is through the Word. The Spirit thus comes from the Father in the Name of the Son, uttering the Word made flesh. He comes, so to speak, as 'formed Spirit' (*filioque*), the Spirit of Christ, so that the term 'quickening Spirit' (πνεῦμα ζωοποιοῦν) can be applied to Christ Himself as well as to the Spirit (John 6.63; 1 Cor. 15.45; 2 Cor. 3.6; 1 Pet. 3.18). Christ as the last Adam is 'quickening Spirit', and so He says: 'The words that I speak unto you they are Spirit and they are Life' (John 6.63). This means that we have to think of the whole relation between the Spirit and the Body in terms of the Word of Christ uttered creatively in the Church through the Spirit, and not simply in terms of the divine cause and a creaturely operation. But in this case the relation between Spirit and Body through the Word involves a relation of calling and address on the part of the Lord the Spirit and an obedience and faith on the part of men. It is acutely personal action. Certainly there takes place here a divine operation bringing the Church into *being*, but that operation is through Christ the Word made flesh and through His uttered Word calling men into obedience and love.

It is through faith that the event takes place, i.e. the actualisation of the Word in the Church and its adaptation to the Word, and thus the compacting of it into a Body as the Body of Christ, the Temple of the Holy Spirit, the Habitation of God.

We may understand this expansive movement from the *soma* to the *pleroma* in another way. Here we recall that the doctrine of the Spirit has Christology for its content (John 14.17, 26; 15.26; 16.13f), so that the doctrine of the Spirit is really Christology (cf. 'the Spirit of Christ', Gal. 4.6; Rom. 8.9; Phil. 1.19; 1 Pet. 1.11) applied to the Church as the Body of Christ. In the Virgin Birth of Jesus Christ the Eternal Word was uttered by the power of the Spirit in the form of the Babe of Bethlehem. The universal Creator Word through whom all things were made and in whom all things cohere (Col. 1.16f; John 1.3f; Heb. 1.3) was incarnated in the infant Jesus, wrapped in swaddling clothes and laid in a manger. The whole Godhead dwelt σωματικῶς in Christ Jesus (Col. 2.9), in the narrow constraint (στενοχωρία) of a particular man—and how straitened He was with that until it was accomplished (Luke 12.50). But as such Jesus Christ was also the New Man, the Last Adam, the Head of a new race gathering up all humanity in Himself (Eph. 1.10; Rom. 5.15f; 1 Cor. 15.21f, 45), and in Him that new humanity pressed toward its universalisation or catholicisation (*pleroma*) in the resurrection of Christ and His ascension to fill all things (Eph. 1.23; 4.10). It was as such that He sent out His Spirit upon the Church begetting it and assuming its existence in space and time into communion with His own existence in the Body which He assumed for Himself in the Incarnation, and determining its form and course in space and time in accordance with His own life and work in the Body. Thus, as Karl Barth has put it, the Incarnation of the Word of God in Jesus Christ is given through the Spirit a 'repetition' (*Wiederholung*) in the historical existence of the Church.[1] This means that at Pentecost the Word of the Gospel is effectually realised in the creation out of the matrix of Israel of a new

[1] *Kirchliche Dogmatik*, 1/2, pp. 135, 136; cf. also p. 302. In his latest volume of the *Kirchliche Dogmatik*, 4/1, pp. 857ff, Barth wisely rejects the concept of 'repetition' and falls back upon a careful use of 'reflection' and 'analogy'. What has led him to do this is the astonishing likeness he finds between Bultmann's conception of the existential repetition of Christ's work in the subjectivity of faith, and the Romanist conception of repetition in the Mass. See also vol. 3/2, pp. 531ff.

soma, the Body of Christ, the Church. But here in this Body there takes place a parallel movement from particularity to universality, for filled with the Spirit of Christ who has ascended to fill all things, the Church is caught up in the movement of *pleroma*. As such it is a kind of first-fruits of the new creation (Jas. 1.18; Rev. 14.4; cf. Rom. 8.23; 1 Cor. 15.20), the new humanity in concentrated form, as it were, pressing out immediately in expansion to the utmost limits. The parallel is so close that it is really impossible to say whether St. Paul is sometimes speaking of the *pleroma* as referring to Christ or His Church. 'He hath put all things under his feet, and gave him to be the head over all things to the church, which is his body, the fulness of him that filleth all in all' (Eph. 1.22f).

On the day of Pentecost St. Peter recalled the Messianic promise that in the last days God would pour out His Spirit upon *all* flesh (Acts 2.17; Joel 2.28). As a matter of fact it was poured out immediately only upon the Church, and yet through the Church it was destined for all men, for the Church is sent out on a mission to all nations teaching and baptising them in the name of the Lord (Matt. 28.19; Mark 16.15f), that they too might receive the promise of the Spirit and be incorporated into the One Body (Acts 2.38f).

This is the point in the movement of *soma* to *pleroma* where we have to see the significance of the Apostolate. On Easter evening with words recalling the promise of Christ to found His Church upon the rock (John 20.23; Matt. 16.19; 18.18), the risen Lord breathed upon the Disciples the Holy Spirit[1] and said: 'As the Father hath sent me, so send I you' (John 20.21). The sending of the Disciples as Apostles is the counterpart to the sending of the Holy Spirit by the Father in the Name of the Son (John 14.26). In Christ as Apostle from God the Father, the Word of God and the Person of Christ are identical (John 3.34f; 5.19f, 33ff; 6.29ff; 7.27f; 8.42f; 10.30ff). He is the God He represents in His own Person: I AM. 'I and my Father are one' (John 10.30). He is the Apostle in the absolute sense (Heb. 3.1). The Apostles, however, are sent to represent Christ in such a way that their persons retreat into the background (1 Cor. 3 and 2 Cor. 4), and yet in such a

---

[1] The relation of the Church of living stones to Christ the Rock is spoken of in terms of οἶκος πνευματικός in 1 Pet. 2.4f. For Paul Christ is πνευματικὴ πέτρα (1 Cor. 10.4) and the Church is σῶμα πνευματικόν (1 Cor. 6.17, 15.44f; Rom. 8.9f).

way that their message, the *kerygma*, is Christ's very own Word. The personal representative of Christ is the Holy Spirit, the *Sāliaḥ*-Spirit, Christ's other Self, as it were, so that of His coming Christ says, 'I will come unto you' (John 14.18). Here we are to think of the Apostles as the chosen vessels appointed to receive the Revelation of Christ, to pass it through their mind, and pass it on to the Church. In the Apostolic Revelation Jesus Christ returns clothed in His Spirit, the Spirit of Truth, and gives Himself to be known and appropriated by the Apostles in His own Spirit, in His own Truth, in His own Light. After Pentecost as the Spirit is poured out upon the Apostles making them into the foundation of the Church, His Body, Christ discloses Himself in greater *pleroma* to them (John 14.25f; 16.12f). He came to fill all things and to fulfil in the Apostles His own Self-revelation and Reconciliation. That is the Apostolic mission. It is not any new revelation or any new interpretation added to it or put upon the objective Revelation in the historical Christ, but the actual unfolding of the Mind of the risen Lord within His Church, the *pleroma* of the incarnational Revelation through His Spirit. The Apostles thus formed the definite medium in our flesh and blood where the unfolding of the Mind of Christ was met by inspired witness and translated into the language of the flesh, the medium, where, as it were, the Revelation of Christ through the Spirit became earthed in the Church as the Body of Christ, became rooted in humanity. The Apostolate expressly formed and shaped for this purpose is the human end of the incarnational Revelation. It is co-ordinated with it and is caught up in its finality and authority.

In this way the Apostles formed the *hinges* of the divine mission, where, so to speak, the vertical mission in the sending of the Son by the Father, is folded out horizontally into history at Pentecost (cf. John 17.9, 13ff). The Apostles are hinges in two senses, as Twelve Disciples, and as Twelve Apostles.

(*a*) As Twelve Disciples they are the hinges between the Old Israel with its Twelve Patriarchs and Tribes, and the New Israel which is reconstituted in them as the Body round the Messiah-King. In this sense the Apostles are the authoritative link between the Old Testament Revelation and the New Testament Revelation. It is on the ground of the Apostolic witness that the Old Testament is subsumed under the New

Testament Revelation, so that the Church is founded on the Apostles and *Prophets*.

(*b*) As Twelve Apostles they are the hinges between the incarnational Revelation objectively given in Christ, and the unfolding of that once and for all in the mind of the Church as the Body of Christ.

That is the twofold Apostolic Mission and it is within that mission and upon it that the Church is founded as upon a Rock. This Church is Apostolic, grounded upon the unrepeatable foundation, a foundation once and for all laid (1 Cor. 3.10f; Eph. 2.20f; cf. 1 Pet. 2.4-9; Matt. 16.13-23). There can be no more laying of foundations, any more than there can be other incarnations or crucifixions of Christ or rebaptism (Heb. 6.6). Because in this primary sense the Apostolate is unrepeatable, it cannot be extended in time on the stage of this world. Rather do we have to do with a perpetually persisting foundation of the Church, and not simply the initial stage of a continuing process. In this sense there can be no talk of Apostolic succession, for the Apostolate cannot be transmitted.

We may understand that in terms of the ascension of Christ. By ascension Christ has withdrawn Himself from the visible succession of history, and at once sends us back to the Apostolic witness to Him, and sends us His Spirit by which He fulfils His own Revelation of Himself. It is as the Church is directed back to the Apostolic witness that the ascended Christ gathers up the Church to Himself and incorporates it into Himself as His Body. The Apostolate thus forms the link in the Body between Christ the Head of the Body and the members of the Body, for their inspired witness (i.e. the New Testament) forms the determinate medium through which the ascended Lord reveals Himself, so that from age to age He ever incorporates the Church into Himself as His Body.

To gather this up so far: When we think of the Church as the Body of Christ we have to think of it in terms of the mission of the Son from the Father which through the Apostolic Foundation is inserted into history reaching out through the ages to the *parousia*. In this whole movement the being and mission of the Church are inseparable. It is the term *body* which above all expresses in the New Testament the interpenetration of being and mission in the concrete reality of the Church. The

New Testament certainly uses many other terms with which to speak of the Church such as people, family, temple, flock, vine, bride, etc., and all must be used to correct and modify each other in our understanding and in any full discussion; but there can be no doubt about the fact that the body is the central and all-important conception, for it is here that the Church is seen to be rooted in the love of God which has over-flowed into the world and embodied itself in our humanity in the Beloved Son, and to be grounded in the crucifixion and in the resurrection of His Body, so that through union with Him in Spirit and Body the Church participates in the divine nature and engages in Christ's ministry of reconciliation.

Before we come to think specifically of the ministry of the Church as the function of the Body of Christ in history, we have to be more precise about the relation between the Church and Christ the Head of the Body. We may do that in four ways, bringing out those aspects of the Body which are important for the doctrine of the ministry.

(1) When we speak of the Church as Christ's Body we are certainly using analogical language, but we are speaking nevertheless of an ontological fact, that is, of a relation of *being* between the Church and Christ. That is very apparent in the use of *agape* to describe the nature of the Church. When we speak of the Church as the Body of Christ we are saying that it is given such union with Christ that it becomes a communion filled and overflowing with the divine love. This love is not to be understood simply in terms of quality but as ontological reality. 'God *is* love. And he that dwells in love, dwells in God, and God in him. . . . As he is, so are we in this world' (1 John 4.16, 17). Or, as St. Paul puts it in a prayer: 'that Christ may dwell in your hearts by faith, that ye being rooted and grounded in love . . . may be filled with all the fulness of God' (Eph. 3.17, 19). Through faith the Church is brought into a relation of being with Christ, so that beyond faith there is an ontological reality upon which the being of the Church is grounded.

In other language from the same Epistle, the Church is grounded in the eternal purpose of love or the divine election that has been actualised in the Beloved Son (Eph. 1.4f). In Him the Church is adopted and gathered up into one Body. Here election is regarded as essentially corporate in nature

29

which has moved into history in Jesus Christ and from whom it moves out into history and is progressively actualised by incorporation into Christ as the concrete embodiment of the divine love. In other words, when St. Paul speaks of the Church as the Body of Christ he is speaking of the ontological reality of its oneness with Christ in love. That oneness is a mystery which reaches back into the eternal ages in the divine *purpose* ($\pi\rho\delta\theta\epsilon\sigma\iota\varsigma$, $\pi\rho\sigma\tau\ell\theta\epsilon\sigma\theta\alpha\iota$) but which He has now *set forth* in history in the mystery of union between Christ and His Church ($\pi\rho\delta\theta\epsilon\sigma\iota\varsigma$, $\pi\rho\sigma\tau\ell\theta\epsilon\sigma\theta\alpha\iota$, see Rom. 8.28; 9.11; Eph. 1.11; 3.11; 2 Tim. 1.9; Rom. 3.25; Eph. 1.9). All that Paul says of the love which the Spirit sheds abroad in our hearts (Rom. 5.5), or of the bond of love which nothing can sever (Rom. 8.35f), is brought to its stark concretion in the term 'Body of Christ' describing the reality in being of the love-union (1 Cor. 6.13f).

The communion of the Spirit thus gives the Church to participate in the concrete embodiment of the Love of God in the Incarnate Son, so that the essential nature and being of the Church as love is its participation in Jesus Christ the New Man. Love in the Church is precisely its participation in the Humanity of Jesus Christ who is the love of God poured out for us and our salvation. The being of the Church as love is its new being in Christ Jesus, and the Church is given this new being as it is grafted into Him. He is the Vine of Truth (to transpose it back into its Hebrew idiom, cf. Jer. 2.21 which lies behind John 15.1f; cf. also Jer. 2.22 and John 15.3, etc.), including the branches. It is ontological reality, for Jesus Christ and His Church form one Body in truth and love (Eph. 2.15f; 4.15, 21f; John 17.17-26; Heb. 2.11; 10.14, etc.).

This is no static reality, however, for it is love in operation, in the fulfilment of the eternal purpose. Here it is apparent that the interpenetration of being and mission constitutes the nature of the Church, so that the Church *is* Church as it participates in the active operation of the divine love. That is particularly clear in the Johannine teaching, for what Jesus has to say about continuing in love and the mission of the Spirit are exactly parallel. 'As the Father has loved me, so have I loved you. Continue ye in my love' (John 15.9). 'As the Father sent me, so send I you. And when Jesus had said this, he breathed on them the Holy Spirit and said unto them: whose soever sins ye remit, they are remitted unto them; and whose soever sins ye retain, they are retained' (John 20.21f). Here the being of the Church in love and the mission of the Church involve one another and both depend on the relation of the Son with the Father, while in John 17 the oneness of the Church with Christ is spoken of as grounded in the oneness of the Father and the Incarnate Son in the life and love of the Godhead.

(2) When St. Paul speaks of the Church as the Body of Christ, He is expressly *distinguishing* the Church from Christ, although the being of the Church is grounded in the oneness of the love between the Father and the Son (John 17.26). In reaching out after ways to express that St. Paul turns to the analogy of marriage again and again (cf. Rom. 7.4; Eph. 5.28f; 1 Cor. 6.13f; 2 Cor. 11.12, etc.) and shows that while the Church is one Body with Christ it is in no sense an extension of His Personality (surely an un-Biblical conception) or an extension of His Incarnation, not to speak of a reincarnation of the Risen Lord. The basic thought here is the relation of the Creator Spirit to the Church who has begotten it and brought it into relation with God in love. It is that which governs the analogy of marriage, which in this context is opened out and made to point quite beyond itself to the mystery of union between Christ and His Church (Eph. 5.28f). In the Pauline doctrine of marriage, 'the work of the man is to explain, to justify the woman; the work of the woman to reveal the man. This is a matter of great importance. When the woman is referred to as her husband's body, it does not mean that she is his extension, but is on the contrary his manner of meeting himself. This in turn reflects on the meaning of the Church as the Body of Christ. She is not Christ continued, the Incarnation continued. One cannot pass without interruption from Christ to the Church. The Cross stands between. In being the Body of Christ, the Church meets her Lord; she does not prolong Him, but she expresses Him here and now. She does not replace Him, but makes Him visible, demonstrates Him without being confounded with Him.'[1]

This way of speaking recalls again the language of Karl Barth when he speaks of the Church as the subjective reality of Revelation. Although, as we have seen, he can speak of the

[1] Ian Muirhead, in review of *Maris et femmes d'après saint Paul*, by J.-J. von Allmen. *Scottish Journal of Theology*, 6, p. 331.

Church in terms of a 'repetition' of the Incarnation, he is careful to qualify his terms. 'The existence of the Church (i.e. as the Body of Christ) involves a repetition of the Incarnation of the Word of God in the Person of Jesus Christ in that area of the rest of humanity which is distinct from the Person of Jesus Christ. The repetition is quite heterogeneous. Yet for all its heterogeneity, it is homogeneous too, although the uniqueness of the objective Revelation forbids us to call it a continuation, prolongation, or extension or the like'.[1]

Through the Communion of the Spirit Christ enters into a relation with the Church in which He adopts the Church and presents it to Himself as His Body, in which He is subjectively present to the Church, not only from without, not only from above, but from beneath and from within.[2] Through the Spirit Christ does not only meet the Church but dwells in it, opens it up and adapts it for Himself in revelation and reconciliation, effectuating its meeting with Himself, so that it finds its true being and true destiny in Him. The Body of Christ thus refers to that sphere within our humanity where Christ not only comes to us in the power of the Spirit but creates an abiding communion with Him where He is to be known through His Word and to be met in love, and where our meeting with Him is actualised and our true destiny is reached in becoming the instrument of His love and in reflecting His glory (1 Cor. 6.11-20; Eph. 5.23-33).

(3) The whole relation between the Church and Christ is governed by the atonement.[3] 'He loved the Church and gave himself for it' (Eph. 5.25). He died to take our place and it is that substitutionary relation which determines the way in which the Church as Body is related to Christ the Saviour of the Body and the Head of the Church (Eph. 5.23f). Here atonement and incorporation belong together, but incorporation into Christ is on the basis of atonement. The incredible fact of the Gospel is that 'He who knew no sin was made sin

---

[1] *Kirchliche Dogmatik* 1/2, p. 235. Barth goes on to speak of the limitation of the Church involved in the concept of the 'body' in a way that corresponds to the *anhypostasis* of Christ's human nature. 'The repetition of the Incarnation of the Word of God in the historical existence of the Church excludes at once any possible autonomy in that existence. The Church lives with Christ as the Body with its Head.'

[2] Cf. *Kirchliche Dogmatik* 1/1, p. 472f; 1/2, p. 233f, 269f.

[3] For a fuller exposition of this see 'The Atonement and the Oneness of the Church', *S.J.T.* 7, pp. 245-269.

for us that we might be made the righteousness of God in him' (2 Cor. 5.21); that 'though he was rich yet for your sakes he became poor, that ye through his poverty might become rich' (2 Cor. 8.9). That is, He took our place that we might take His place before God. And yet when Christ presents the Church to the Father as His own Body it is on the ground of the fact that He took its place. As the Body of this Christ the Church is the sphere where that substitution is actualised within history, so that only as it lets Christ take its place, only as it yields place to Him, is it His Body. Baptism is thus the Sacrament of substitution and the Lord's Supper the Sacrament through which the Church, as the congregation of sinners, continues to deny self and take up His Cross until He come.[1]

St. Matthew tells us that it was in founding His Church that Jesus began to speak to His Disciples about His crucifixion (Matt. 16.21f). When Peter the rock objected, Jesus rebuked him calling him an offence or a stone of stumbling. The foundation of the Church demanded not only His crucifixion but radical self-denial on the part of the Disciples on the ground of the Cross and the displacement which it involved. 'If any man will come after me, let him deny himself and take up his cross and follow me' (Matt. 16.24). In later years St. Peter remembered he had been a stone of stumbling and a rock of offence (1 Pet. 2.8), and warned those being baptised into Christ (1 Pet. 1.2f, 22f) against his own mistake. The Church is grounded upon redemption with the precious Blood of Christ (1 Pet. 1.18f) and those baptised into the Church are built up on that foundation as living stones into a spiritual house, a holy priesthood (1 Pet. 2.4f).

That is the way in which the Church becomes the Body of Christ, that being baptised into His death it might be baptised out of itself and gathered into His Name. That is why Baptism is the Sacrament of substitution through which we find shelter in the Name of Another, in the Name of Jesus Christ. The Church that is baptised no longer belongs to itself. It belongs to Christ as His Body, 'for he loved the church and gave himself for it that he might sanctify and cleanse it with the washing of water by the word (ἐν ῥήματι = the baptismal formula? but cf.

---

[1] That judgment in the House of God is involved in the sacramental life of the Church is particularly clear in the whole of 1 Peter. See especially 4.12-18 and cf. 1 Cor. 3.12. With 1 Pet. 4.17, cf. Ezek. 9.6; Jer. 25.29.

John 15.2) that he might present it unto himself a glorious church, not having spot or wrinkle, nor any such thing; but that it should be holy and without blemish' (Eph. 5.24f).

(4) The fourth point we have to note in the relation of the Church to Christ is the *conformity* between the Body and the Head of the Body. Jesus Christ had a Baptism with which He was baptised (Mark 10.38f)[1] and He has given His Church to share in His Baptism, so that in Baptism the Church is grafted together with Christ in His death and resurrection (Rom. 6.4f). That is the doctrine of the One Baptism which, as Calvin puts it, 'Christ has in common between Himself and His Church' (*Instit.* 4.15.6; *Comm. on Eph.* 4.5).[2] As there is One Spirit so through One Baptism there is One Body in which there takes place in the Church, as it were, a spiritual reduplication or fulfilment of the birth, life, death and resurrection of Christ. That Baptism, however, is not over when it is done. In the Marcan account Jesus says, 'I have a baptism with which I am being baptised', where His Baptism refers to His whole existence as the Servant of the Lord reaching out to its fulfilment.[3] The Church that is baptised with Christ's Baptism assumes like Him, the form of a Servant (Phil. 2.7), working out the salvation God works in it (Phil. 2.17). Thus its faith takes the form of θυσία καὶ λειτουργία (Phil. 2.17; cf. 1.29). It has not only died and risen with Him, but continues 'to bear about in its body the dying of the Lord Jesus that the life also of Jesus might be made manifest in our mortal flesh' (2 Cor. 4.10f). To put that the other way round, as St. Paul does too, the Church through Baptism into the death of Christ is made to grow together with Him (Rom. 6.5, σύμφυτοι γεγόναμεν) so that in a very real sense Christ comes to be formed within the Church giving it conformity with Him (Gal. 4.19; Phil. 3.10, 21; Rom. 6.3f; 8.29; 12.1f, etc.). Because that is so, in a true doctrine of the Church and ministry the Christological pattern must be made to appear in the form and order of the Church. That applies particularly to the function of the Church, for in Baptism it is inserted into the functioning of the Body of Christ, into His servant-ministry. 'Whosoever will be great among you, let him be your minister; and whosoever will be chief

---

[1] See J. A. T. Robinson, 'The One Baptism', *S.J.T.*, 6, pp. 257-274.
[2] See R. S. Wallace, *Calvin's Doctrine of the Word and Sacrament*, p. 175f.
[3] See J. A. T. Robinson, op. cit., p. 259.

among you let him be your servant; even as the Son of Man came not to be ministered unto but to minister and to give his life a ransom for many' (Matt. 20.26f). And so at the Last Supper, as the Fourth Gospel tells us, when Jesus washed the feet of the disciples recalling their Baptism, He spoke of consecrating them into His ministry after His own pattern (John 13.4-17).

It is now clear that, as the ministry is grounded upon the whole relation of the Church to Christ, the doctrine of the ministry must be formulated in terms of the Christological pattern (ὑπόδειγμα). In other words, because He is pleased to use the Church as His Body and to use it in His ministry of reconciliation, we must think of the ministry of the Church as correlative to the ministry of Christ. The ministry of the Church is thus the function of the Body appropriate to it as the Body of which He is the Head and Saviour (Eph. 5.23). Or to put it the other way round, as the Body of which He is the Head the Church participates in His ministry by serving Him in history where it is sent by Him in fulfilment of His ministry of reconciliation, in the renewal of the world and the extension of His Kingdom.

What are we to understand by the Church's *participation* in the ministry of Christ?

Because the Church is formed by One Spirit into One Body with Christ, the participation of the Church in the ministry of Christ is *primarily corporate*. Thus the ministry of the Church refers primarily to the royal priesthood which pertains to the whole membership of Christ's Body.[1] That has been very aptly put by Dr J. A. T. Robinson in a recent work. 'All that is said of the ministry in the New Testament is said not of individuals nor of some apostolic college or "essential ministry" but of the whole Body, whatever the differentiation of function within it. This follows because the whole life of Christ is given to the Church to be possessed *in solidum*: the Spirit, the New Life, the Priesthood, everything, belongs to each as it belongs to all. In Pauline language this is expressed by saying that

---

[1] The expression 'priesthood of all believers' is an unfortunate one as it carries with it a ruinous individualism. 'Priest' in the singular is never found in the NT applied to the believer, any more than 'king' in the singular. In the singular these words could only apply to Christ Himself. Like the term 'saints' used only collectively in the NT, 'priests' and 'kings' apply corporately to the whole membership of the Church.

Christ's life is now lived and given "Bodywise" (*Somatikos*), not individually but corporately, so that the fulness of God now resides in Him as it resides at the same time in us His members (Col. 2.9f).'[1] Certainly this corporate ministry involves a membering within the One Body due to the diverse and special gifts of the Spirit, given for the edification and growth of the Body into the fulness of Christ the Head (1 Cor. 12.1ff; Rom. 12.1ff; Eph. 4.1ff). But within the royal priesthood we have to think of a special qualification of priesthood resulting in an ordained ministry within the Church. Because this special qualification of priesthood is within the corporate priesthood of the whole Body it has to be given primarily a corporate or collegiate expression. That fact, the corporate nature of the Church's participation in Christ's ministry, is extremely important for it affects our views both of order within the Church and of the continuity of the ministry.

This corporate ministry of the Church and the ministry of Christ are related to each other, *not as the less to the greater, not as the part to the whole*, but *as the participation of the Church in the whole ministry of Christ.*

Sometimes the ministry of the Church and the ministry of Christ are related in different degrees of authority and power, and in degrees of validity, but then the qualitative difference between the ministry of Christ and the ministry of the Church is blurred by a comparison involving quantitative or juridical distinctions. But the one fixed point from which we cannot get away is that Christ's ministry is absolutely unique. *Sacerdotium Christi non est in genere.*

Sometimes a distinction is drawn, especially by would-be 'Catholics', between certain functions of Christ regarded as primary, unique, and non-transferable, and other functions which can be transferred by His authority to His chosen representatives and through them be extended in the continuing ministry of the Church. This is a view that by-passes the resurrection and the ascension and seeks to ground the ministry of the Church entirely on the historical Jesus, but it operates also with an un-Biblical way of speaking. The New Testament does not draw such distinctions but boldly speaks of the Church as participating in the whole ministry of Christ. He fulfils His ministry in a unique and unrepeatable way, but the Church's

[1] *The Historic Episcopate*, edited by Kenneth M. Carey, p. 14.

36

ministry is to be undertaken with reference not to a part but to the whole of His ministry. Christ is Prophet, Priest, and King, and the Church's ministry is correlatively prophetic, priestly, and kingly. The ministry of the Church is in no sense an extension of the ministry of Christ or a prolongation of certain of His ministerial functions. That is the view that leads to very wrong notions of Eucharistic Sacrifice as an extension of Christ's own priestly sacrifice in the Eucharist, and to wrong notions of priesthood as the prolongation of His Priesthood in the ministry: and behind it all lies the notion of the Church as an extending or prolonging of the Incarnation, and sometimes, as in certain Roman expositions, there even lurks the heretical idea of the reincarnation of Christ in the Church through the Spirit regarded as the soul of the Church.

It is not easy to state precisely the relation between the ministry of the Church and the ministry of Christ described as participation. But two things should be quite clear. On the one hand, there can be *no relation of identity* in part or in whole between the ministry of the Church and the ministry of Christ. It is very often some form of this identity that lies behind the so-called 'Catholic' view of the ministry. On the other hand, the ministry of the Church is *not another ministry* different from the ministry of Christ, or separable from it. It is the element of separation that lies so often behind the so-called 'sectarian' view of the Church or ministry. The Church that is baptised with Christ's Baptism and drinks His Cup engages in His ministry in a way appropriate to the redeemed and appropriate to the Body. Christ exercises His ministry in a way appropriate to the Redeemer and appropriate to the Head of the Body. Thus the relation between Christ's ministry and the Church's ministry is described in the New Testament in terms of the relation between the Head and the members of the Body, between the Lord and the servant, between the Householder and the steward, between the King and the herald: from beginning to end it is a relation of subordination and obedience. The Church participates in Christ's ministry by *serving* Him who is Prophet, Priest, and King.

The ministry of the Church is related to the ministry of Christ in such a way that in and through the ministry of the Church it is always Christ Himself who is at work, nourishing, sustaining, ordering, and governing His Church on earth.

37

Through His Spirit He commands and enables the Church to minister in His Name, to preach Christ crucified and risen, to declare the forgiveness of sins, and call all men to be reconciled to God, but it is the Lord Himself who is present in the midst of His Church as the Word made flesh making the preaching of the Gospel effectual as Word and Power of God. Through His Spirit He commands and enables the Church to administer the Sacraments of Baptism and the Lord's Supper, but it is the Lord Himself who is present in the midst of the Church as our High Priest who cleanses the Church in His own Blood, feeds it with Himself, blesses it with His Spirit, renews it in the power of His resurrection, and presents it as His own Body to the Father. Through His Spirit He commands and enables the Church to be ordered in His Name, appointing to each his function as a member in His One Body, so that in a ministry involving diversity of operations and differences of administration, the Church is built up in the unity of the faith as a Temple of God, but it is the Lord Himself who is present through the One Spirit as King governing the Church and using it as the instrument of His Gospel in the extension of His Kingdom and the renewal of the world. Throughout the whole prophetic, priestly, and kingly ministry of the Church, it is Christ Himself who presides as Prophet, Priest, and King, but He summons the Church to engage in *His* ministry by witness (μαρτυρία), by stewardship (οἰκονομία), and by service (διακονία).

In all this it is apparent that the Church so participates in the ministry of Christ that the whole direction of the Church's ministry is determined by a movement from the Head of the Body downward to the members of the Body, from the ascended Lord downward to His Church. That means that the Church's ministry is God-given and participates in the motion of grace from God to man, and ministers in the same direction as grace moves, but it also means that the ministry of the Church is exercised only within the irreversible relationship of Lord and servant, Head and Body, in subordination, and in entire conformity, to the Kingdom of Christ.

Out of this there emerge two fundamental principles for a doctrine of the ministry.

(*a*) The essential motion of the Church's ministry must be correlative to the whole incarnational movement of Christ described in the New Testament as His *descent* and *ascent*, His *katabasis* and His *anabasis*. In its most comprehensive sweep that refers to His *katabasis* into our mortal humanity at His birth and His *anabasis* wearing our resurrected humanity in His ascension, but within that whole movement it refers to His *katabasis* in death and His *anabasis* in resurrection.[1] The nadir of that whole movement of descent and ascent was His substitutionary death on the Cross. Correlative to that, the ministry of the Church describes a movement of counterpoint to His descent and to His ascent and in that order.

The ministry of the Church, therefore, is grounded upon a reception of the Christ who descends into the midst and then, on the ground of His substitutionary atonement in which He at once takes our place and unites us to Himself, the motion of the ministry is to be described as an oblation of thanksgiving and worship, correlative to Christ's ascension or oblation[2] of Himself in which He presents the Church as His own Body to the Father. That is why, for example, in the Epistle to the Ephesians Paul grounds the doctrine of the ministry in the gifts of the Spirit sent down by the ascended Lord when He has completed His movement of descent and ascent (Eph. 4.7ff). Thus through the Spirit the Church participates not only in the whole growth of Christ from birth to the full stature of manhood but in His descent into death and in His ascent into the heavenly places. That is why too when the Epistle to the Hebrews speaks of our participation in the heavenly calling it bids us consider Jesus as the Apostle and High Priest of our confession, i.e. as the One sent from God to man who as such opens up the way from man to God. The Godward movement reposes upon the manward movement. Of that the ministry of the Church is essentially a reflex.

Nothing could be more wrong than to reverse the movement of descent and ascent into a movement of ascent and descent, for that would be to enunciate a doctrine of the ministry as

[1] It seems to me entirely wrong to explain passages like John 3.13 and Ephesians 4.9f in terms of the myth of the Heavenly or Primal Man, as is done by Bultmann, Käsemann and Schlier, when this language is indigenous to Judaism and Christianity. It derives in the first place from the habit of speaking of ascent into the Holy Place and descent from it, and in the second place from Baptism. The explanation of the passages in question lies in the application of these terms to the whole incarnational movement. It is the language of Jewish liturgy, not gnostic mythology, that is employed here.

[2] In Hebrew the terms for ascension and oblation are the same: עָלָה.

Pelagian movement grounded upon an Adoptionist Christology and upon a heathen notion of atonement as act of man upon God, involving a correspondingly heathen notion of Eucharistic Sacrifice.[1]

(*b*) Within this whole movement of descent and ascent in which the Church as the Body of Christ participates in His ministry, the relation between the Head of the Body and the members of the Body governs the mode of representation. That means that the ministry of the Church is not to be thought of as a function of the people or of their delegates. The ministry of the Church is not democratically grounded and built up from the members of the Church so as to represent them before God. Certainly the ministry in the Church is an expression of the ministry of the Church, so that all who exercise that ministry are inseparable from the Church and have a relation of mutuality and reciprocity with the members of the Church, as Paul indicates so clearly in his own relationships with the Corinthian Church, for example (2 Cor. 1); but Paul never speaks once of himself as being the representative of the Church before God and as acting on their behalf toward God, and therefore as responsible to the Church for his action toward God on their behalf.

On the contrary, the ministry represents the Head of the Body in His ministry for the members of the Body, and only represents the Body as the Body is the instrument of the Head of the Body. It is from above downward that ministerial representation is grounded and not from below upward. But because the ministry of Christ is on behalf of the Body, on the ground of what Christ has done for the Body, the ministry in the Church is also on behalf of the Body. It was because Paul acted on behalf of Christ (ὑπὲρ Χριστοῦ) that He could speak of himself as acting on behalf of His Body, the Church (ὑπὲρ τοῦ σώματος αὐτοῦ, ὅ ἐστιν ἡ ἐκκλησία 2 Cor. 5.20f; Col. 1.24f). Paul is above all a minister of the Gospel (Col. 1.23) and as such he is a minister of the Church (Col. 1.25), but this ministry is defined as 'according to the dispensation (*oikonomia*) of God given to me for you (εἰς ὑμᾶς) to fulfil the word of God'

[1] It is rather ironical for Scotsmen to find that William Milligan's Biblical exposition of the Priesthood of Christ (*The Ascension and Heavenly Priesthood of our Lord*) combined with the Pelagian element of atonement in the teaching of MacLeod Campbell (*The Nature of the Atonement*) should yield the view of Moberley in his *Ministerial Priesthood*!

(Col. 1.25). In terms of the Corinthian Epistle Paul speaks of himself as the servant of the Church for Jesus' sake (2 Cor. 4.5, 11, διὰ 'Ιησοῦν). It cannot be emphasised too much that the ministry is grounded upon the gifts of the ascended Lord and Head of the Church, and therefore the ministerial representatives of Christ within the Church and to the Church receive their commission or orders not from the Church but for it, for their commission has its sole right in the gift given by Christ and in offering the gifts given by Christ in Word and Sacrament. Because the ministry is grounded on the gift of the Spirit and through the Spirit on the gift of Christ Himself to the Church in the Eucharist and is, as we shall see, validated by His real presence, the devolution of the ministry through representatives of the Church or ministerial succession cannot be given more than the signification of a sign.[1] The historical succession of ecclesiastical representatives is not identical with the real succession of the corporate participation of the Church in the ministry of Christ, and can only point to it and signify it, important and indeed essential as that succession on the plane of history is. The reason for this lies in the very nature of the representation. As we saw in the case of the Apostles the representation was not a personal representation involving any element of identity. Christ is Himself the Apostle in the sense that He represents God not only in His ministry but in His own Person, for He *is* God. The Apostles represent Christ in a secondary sense, such that their persons retreat into the background. It was not Paul or Peter that was crucified, the Apostle is only δοῦλος τοῦ Χριστοῦ, and the law of his representation may well be taken from the lips of John the Baptist: 'He must increase, I must decrease' (John 3.30).[2] The Apostle ministers in such a way that his person does not in any sense mediate between God and man but in such a way that in his ministry it is Christ Himself who acts through His Spirit, who is Himself the only Apostle and Bishop of our souls (1 Pet. 2.25).

All this raises for us the necessity for a reconsideration of the nature of the continuity of the Church's ministry. If we are to regard this in terms of the continuous function of the Church

---

[1] I owe this way of putting it to an unpublished paper by the late Rev. Dr F. W. Camfield.
[2] See 'A Study in New Testament Communication', *S.J.T.* 3, pp. 298ff.

as the Body of Christ in history, then we will have to face two fundamental issues.

(1) What is the relation of the historical continuity in the Church to the resurrection? And here the Apostles must guide our thinking, for they were given their function to perform as eyewitnesses of the resurrection and to carry out their ministry in founding the Church in the perspective of the resurrection and ascension. Thus the Apostolic norm will be determinative in our answer to the question of continuity. But it should be clear at once that the Church founded upon the Apostles cannot construct a doctrine of the ministry or of historical succession in the ministry that by-passes either the resurrection or the ascension. If the ministry of the Church is the function of the Body of Christ, then we have to think of that in terms of His risen Body, and of the relation of the resurrection to history.

(2) What is the relation between ministerial succession and the corporate functioning of the Body of Christ? Does continuity rest on a line of priestly succession or of ecclesiastical representatives, presbyteral or episcopal, or both? Or does it rest primarily on baptismal incorporation into the Body of Christ crucified and risen and baptismal insertion into the functioning of that Body in history? If the ministry of the Church is primarily corporate, the ministry of the whole Body, then are there any theological reasons which insist that presbyteral or episcopal succession must devolve on individuals only? The corporate priesthood of the Church would seem to demand above all a notion of corporate episcopate, and would seem to rule out the radical individualism that lurks in so many mediaeval and modern views of the episcopate.

Rather shall we have to think of a threefold continuity: (1) of baptismal incorporation into Christ and of the priesthood of the One Body; (2) of the continuity of order as the special qualification of priesthood arising out of the Word and Sacraments; and (3) of episcopal continuity as the ecclesiastical sign in the One Church of continuity in unity.

III

THE TIME OF THE CHURCH

IN the doctrine of the Church as the Body of Christ everything turns upon the fact of the resurrection of Jesus Christ in Body and His ascension in the fulness of His Humanity. That is very apparent today in the contemporary discussion of eschatology, for eschatology properly speaking is the application of Christology to the Kingdom of Christ and to the work of the Church in history. It is because we are united to Christ who is bone of our bone and flesh of our flesh, and participate in the risen Humanity of Christ so that we are bone of His bone and flesh of His flesh (Eph. 5.30), that eschatology is so essential to our faith and life from day to day. Union with Christ means union with the Christ who rose again from the dead, who ascended to the right hand of God the Father, and who will come again; and therefore union with Him here and now carries in its heart the outreach of faith toward the resurrection of the dead and the renewal of heaven and earth at the Second Advent of Christ. The crucial issue in eschatology concerns the Humanity of the risen Christ, and our participation in His Humanity through Word and Sacrament in the Church.

This is a supremely important question today, the point where our deepest divergences come clearly to the surface. Are we to take the Humanity of the risen Jesus seriously or not? Or are we to teach a docetic view of the risen and ascended Jesus? If in a previous generation we had to do battle for the Humanity of the historical Jesus, today we have to do battle for the Humanity of the risen Jesus ascended to the right hand of God the Father Almighty. If Jesus Christ is not risen in Body, then salvation is not actualised in the same sphere of reality in which we are, and we are yet in our sins (1 Cor. 15.17). If Jesus Christ is not ascended in the fulness of His Humanity, then we have no anchor within the veil and there is no hope for us men and women of flesh and blood (Heb. 6.19f; Col. 1.27). To demythologise the ascension (which means, of course, that it must first of all be mythologised) is to dehumanise

43

Christ, and to dehumanise Christ is to make the Gospel of no relevance to humanity, but to turn it into an inhospitable and inhuman abstraction.

Is this not why our churches today often appear so inhospitable because they have lost something, as it were, of the flesh and blood of Jesus Christ? It is only too easy for a church to become an inhuman institution, even if it is an institution of grace, if it operates with a docetic Christology. That may readily happen among 'Catholics' who operate with a doctrine of the Church as *corpus mysticum*, for it produces its dialectical counterpart in a rationalised ecclesiastical institution.[1] It may happen just as readily among 'Liberals' who operate with a doctrine of the Church as the embodiment and expression of Christian ideals, for it produces its counterpart in a secularised society where the scientific reason enslaves the spirit. Mysticism and rationalism, sacramentalism and institutionalism, always go very readily together whether in their 'Catholic' or in their 'Protestant' forms—and in both man is starved for the sheer Humanity of the Son of God.

Against these abstractions the teaching of the New Testament that the Church is the Body of the living Christ stands out in sharp contrast. Here we are concerned very much with the Humanity of Jesus. 'We are members of his body, of his flesh and of his bones' (Eph. 5.30). This is the strongest possible emphasis upon the fact that in the resurrection of Christ and in the Church's participation in Him the purpose of God in creation is brought to its fulfilment. This fulfilment is no abrogation of its creatureliness but on the contrary a restoration of its creaturely reality which had been impaired by sin. Far from being a docetic concept 'the Body of Christ' (unlike the *'corpus mysticum'* which is an abstraction) means that our creaturely humanity is not transcended or transmuted or transsubstantiated but is fully substantiated as creaturely humanity in the creature-Creator relation.

The Pauline concept of the 'spiritual body' ($\sigma\hat{\omega}\mu\alpha\ \pi\nu\epsilon\upsilon\mu\alpha\tau\iota\kappa\acute{o}\nu$) does not mean a spiritualised body, as if it were less body because it has become spiritual. The 'spiritual man' ($\pi\nu\epsilon\upsilon\mu\alpha\tau\iota\kappa\grave{o}\varsigma\ \acute{\alpha}\nu\theta\rho\omega\pi o\varsigma$) is no less man because he is spiritual, but on the contrary, far more man because through the Spirit he participates in the real Humanity of Jesus Christ, who is more fully Man than any other man, and who is above all the humanising

[1] See additional note (1), p. 62.   44

Man, the Man through whom all who believe in Him are humanised, and restored through atonement to true and perfect humanity. As Adam became man through the breath of God, so sinful man becomes man again through the Spirit of God breathed upon him by the risen Christ (John 20.22). The Church is σῶμα πνευματικόν, and as such is the New Man (Eph. 2.15) and within the Church those who are baptised into Christ are 'one man' (Gal. 3.28) for they have 'put on Christ' (Gal. 3.27), or 'put on the new man' (Eph. 4.24). In the Body of Christ, through whom all things were made, man is restored to the full reality of his humanity as creature reflecting the glory of God because here by the Creator Spirit or the live-giving Spirit (1 Cor. 15.45; 2 Cor. 3.6; John 6.63) he is united to Christ in His Humanity. The Church is Body of Christ because, in the striking expression of Calvin, it is renewed and nourished by His 'vivifying flesh'.

But right away, as we think of the Church in terms of the real and actual Humanity of Christ, 'of his flesh and of his bones' (Eph. 5.30) we are faced with the fact of the ascension. Jesus Christ who rose again from the dead in His full Humanity has withdrawn His Body from us, out of the visible succession of history, and He waits until the day when He will come again in Body to judge and to renew the world. And yet after His ascension the Lord has poured out His Spirit upon the Church giving it, while still within on-going history, to participate in the power of His resurrection. On the one hand, then, the Church through the Spirit is joined to the Body of the risen Christ and is One Body with Him; but on the other hand, Christ has removed His Body from us so that we have to think of the relation of the Church to the risen Body of Christ in terms of the distance of the ascension and the nearness of His *parousia* in Glory. There is an eschatological reserve in the relation of our union with Christ, an eschatological lag waiting for the last Word or the final Act of God. There is an element of pure immediacy in the Church's relation to the risen Body of Christ so that His *parousia* is a presence here and now through the Spirit. But there is also an element in the Church's relation to the risen Body of Christ which from our experience and our understanding is still in arrears and awaits the divine fulfilment. Christ has distanced His Body from us and yet through His Spirit He has come and filled the Church with His own Self.

45

In one sense, then, the Church is already One Body with Christ—that has once for all taken place in the crucifixion, resurrection, and in Pentecost—and yet the Church is still to become One Body. Between the 'already One Body' and the 'still to become One Body' we have the doctrine of the ascension and advent of Christ, the ascension reminding us that the Church is other than Christ, while sanctified together with Him; the advent reminding us that the Church in its historical pilgrimage is under the judgment of the impending advent, while already justified in Him. Thus the Church is summoned to look beyond its historical forms in this world to the day when Christ will change the body of our humiliation and make it like unto the Body of His Glory (Phil. 3.21).

This eschatological relation of immediacy and reserve, so strong in the Epistles of the New Testament, is not easy to state precisely because it involves a twofold relation in which the sacramental and the eschatological are inseparable. On the one hand, New Testament eschatology envisages a relation between the new creation and the old creation here and now. Through the Spirit the Church on earth and in empirical history is already participant in the new creation which has overtaken it. Because the Church is at once in the old creation and in the new creation the advent of Christ in Glory is inevitably imminent, for the new creation is always knocking at the door of the old, and the new wine is always breaking the old wine-skins. On the other hand, Christian eschatology envisages a relation between the present and the future which is just as decisive and inescapable as the ascension. 'Now we are the sons of God, and it doth not yet appear what we shall be: but we know that, when he shall appear, we shall be like him, for we shall see him as he is' (1 John 3.2).

The New Testament teaching about the Church as the Body of Christ enshrines both these aspects of the eschatological relation. Indeed it is precisely the conjunction of these two aspects of eschatology in the doctrine of the Church that is so significant, for it means that the Church is so united to the risen Humanity of Christ that within the Church the new creation is a concrete reality reaching out through the ages of history to the *parousia* and so within the Church we are given a new orientation to the succession of time on the stage of this sinful world. The Church as the Body of Christ is the sphere

46

on earth and within history where through the Spirit the redemption of the body and the redemption of time anticipate the *parousia*.

We may illustrate that from the Marcan account of the healing of the paralytic in chapter two. When the paralysed man was let down through the roof into the room where Jesus was preaching, He said to the sick man: 'Son thy sins be forgiven thee' (Mark 2.5), and then waiting for a few moments, He said to him again: 'Arise, and take up thy bed, and go thy way into thine house' (Mark 2.11). Here the word ἐγείρειν is used in apposition to ἀφιέναι (Mark 2.9; Luke 5.23; Matt. 9.5)[1] and the account clearly intends us to see the theological significance of the fact that forgiveness of sins and resurrection of the body belong together as two parts of a whole. The resurrection of the paralysed man is not only a demonstration of the power of forgiveness but is part of its complete eventuation. The raising up of the sick man reveals that the Word of forgiveness on the lips of the Son of Man *on earth* is no mere word but ἐξουσία: 'that ye may know that the Son of Man hath power on earth to forgive sins' (Mark 2.10). It would appear too that the Marcan narrative, written for the use of the Church, intends us in the light of the two moments, the moment of forgiveness and the moment of miraculous healing, to see also the relation between the moment of the crucifixion of Jesus and the moment of His resurrection, the time of the Gospel of the Cross and the time of the resurrection of the body. As in this miracle the actual healing of the paralysed man has already taken place in the Word of forgiveness and only needs the second Word of the Son of Man for it to be made manifest to all, so the work of our salvation is already fully accomplished in what Christ has done for us, and only needs His coming again and the unveiling or apocalypse that it involves to make it manifest to all. The raising of the sick man in body did not add anything to the Word of forgiveness, but it was nevertheless the Word of forgiveness in full and complete event.

The Church of Jesus Christ lives between those two moments

[1] The word ἐγείρω is not used in profane Greek either of raising the dead or raising the sick. These meanings are peculiar to Biblical Greek. Ἐγείρω is preferred by the New Testament to ἀνίστημι for speaking of the raising of the dead. The use of this same word for the raising up of the sick indicates that the New Testament regards miraculous healings as coming within the sphere and power of the resurrection of Christ. His resurrection evidences itself before hand in signs and wonders such as this in Mark 2.

47

or events, between the crucifixion of Jesus Christ proclaimed as the Word of divine forgiveness, and the resurrection of the body promised at the *parousia*. But the Church is not left to be simply suspended in that duality, for along with the Gospel of forgiveness it is given to taste already the good Word of God and the powers of the age to come (Heb. 6.5): and that is the part played by the Sacraments of the Gospel. The Sacraments span the two moments and are ordinances of Christ belonging to the eschatological reserve between the moment of the First Advent and the moment of Final Advent. The Sacraments do not add anything to the Word of forgiveness but they are that Word in complete and full event. They are the ordinances in which as far as possible, while yet remaining within empirical history, we may anticipate the resurrection of the body. It is in the Sacraments above all, therefore, that the Church called into being by the Word of the Gospel of forgiveness really becomes the Body of Christ reaching out to the *parousia*. In and through the Sacraments, therefore, we are given our clearest understanding of the participation of the Church in the redemption of the body and the redemption of time.

There is a significant passage in *The Shepherd* of Hermas (3.10-13) which speaks of a vision he had of the Church as a very old lady sitting on a chair, the *Ecclesia presbytera*, he called her. Then he looked again and saw that though her body and her hair were old her face was getting younger—the *Ecclesia neotera*. He looked a third time and though her hair was white she had altogether recovered her youth, and was quite young, very joyful and beautiful. That is the Biblical doctrine of the Church. In the fifth chapter of Ephesians St. Paul speaks too of the Church as an old lady wrinkled and spotted but she is baptised by Christ and is presented to Him as a young virgin without spot or wrinkle or any blemish (Eph. 5.27; 2 Cor. 11.2). Essentially the same idea is found in 2 Corinthians 4 where St. Paul speaks of our bearing about the dying of the Lord Jesus in our bodies that the life also of Jesus might be made manifest in our mortal flesh, for if the old man perishes the inward man is renewed day by day (2 Cor. 4.10-16). In other words, the Church is corporeal reality in this world and yet through the Spirit the same Church already participates in the new creation. Even though it is involved in the space and

48

time of this world and this age, the life of the Church gets younger and younger because in Christ it is redeemed from the bondage and decay that characterise this world and this age. That is why to speak of the Church as the Body of Christ is to speak of it as the sphere within history where through the Spirit the redemption of the body and the redemption of time anticipate the *parousia*.

This relation of redemption to space and time is of prime importance for the doctrine of the Church and its ministry. Behind it all lies the fact of the Incarnation which tells us that the Eternal Son of God has become flesh, has embodied Himself within the creation which through the sin of man has suffered estrangement and decay and has assumed it into union with Himself. But it also tells us that the Eternal Son has entered our temporal existence with all its contingency, relativity, and transience and has united it to His own eternity. Certainly that assumption or union involved the most passionate tension for Him, revealed in all its horror in Golgotha, but the resurrection and the ascension mean that He has overcome the contradiction and tension and has carried through His union with our creaturely existence and our time into a new creation in which the whole purpose of God in creation is fully realised, and in which our temporality is redeemed out of contingency and relativity and made fully real in union with His own eternity. In the resurrection and ascension our human existence and our human time, without being annihilated or disrupted, are transformed and recreated and are taken up into abiding union with God. The Church, as the Body of this risen and ascended Christ, participates in a reality of creation and time beyond all threat of decay and transience. Through the Word and Sacraments that is a present reality within the Church on earth and in history, so that even on earth and within on-going history the Church is the Body of the risen and ascended Christ. The supernatural life of Christ flows into the Church giving it a new relation to space and time as we know them in our fallen world. To describe that Paul uses the words οἰκοδομή and αὔξησις where he thinks of the flow of the Church's new life as against the stream of decay and of the structure of the Church as erected downward from the coping stone (Eph. 2.20f; 4.15f; Col. 2.19). Here too both οἰκοδομή and αὔξησις are thought into each other in order to

49

modify each other for it takes both in conjunction to express the movement of the Church in space and time, and so to describe its relation to structure and history. It is that conjunction of οἰκοδομή and αὔξησις that yields the doctrine of order.

We must pause to consider this more fully, thinking first of the Church's relation to time, and then of its relation to space.

(1) Time as we know it in our world from day to day is bound up with creation. It is the time of creaturely being, but for us men it is above all the lifetime of man, time in terms of human action and decision and history. But this is what Brunner has called 'crumbling time' (*die zerbröckelnde Zeit*)[1] for as we know and experience it, it is the time of our fallen world which is marked by decay and corruption and above all by sinful history. It is sin-impregnated and guilt-laden time, time under judgment, and therefore time that passes irreversibly away into vanity and death, irreversibly because we can no more put the clock back than we can undo sin and expiate guilt. It is within this time that the Eternal Son of God became incarnate and from within this time that He rose again in body out of death. God did not suffer Him to see corruption (Acts 2.31). The resurrection of Jesus was historical event, but there can be no historiography of the forty days of the resurrection, for the New Man breaks through the limitations of our crumbling time and does not come within what the secular historian as such with his methods and canons of credibility can establish as history. It breaks through that, however, just because it is fully real, historical happening, so real that it does not belong to the decaying, illusory history of this fallen world, but is permanently real, resisting corruption and fleeting contingency. Here in the resurrection of Christ there emerges new time which is permanently real and which is continuous reality flowing against the stream of crumbling time.

That is the time of Jesus Christ risen from the dead, the new time of the Kingdom of God, but it is also the time of the Church as the Body of Christ. That is why St. Paul speaks of the life of the Church as flowing against the stream of decay, for 'old things are passed away and all things are become new' (2 Cor. 5.17). The baptised Church is born again and gets younger and younger, and therefore its function within the on-going

[1] See 'The Christian Understanding of Time', *S.J.T.*, 4, p. 10.

time of this age that passes away is to 'redeem the time' (Eph. 5.16). 'Wherefore, awake thou that sleepest, and arise from the dead, and Christ shall give thee light. See then that ye walk circumspectly, not as fools but as wise, redeeming the time because the days are evil' (ἐξαγοραζόμενοι τὸν καιρόν, ὅτι οἱ ἡμέραι πονηραί εἰσιν—Eph. 5.14f). A similar passage is found in Romans, where Paul says: 'And knowing the time (εἰδότες τὸν καιρόν), it is high time (ὥρα ἤδη) to awake out of sleep (ἐξ ὕπνου ἐγερθῆναι), for now is our salvation nearer than when we believed' (Rom. 13.11f). Because the Church is involved in this new time, real time that is continuous within history, and resists its contingency and decay, the life and work of the Church have to be interpreted against the rhythm and pattern of secular history. The Church that is risen with Christ cannot allow itself to be lulled to sleep in the flow of time (cf. Matt. 25.1ff; 2 Pet. 3.1ff), but must rouse itself (ἐγείρειν), keep awake and keep vigil (γρηγορεῖν, ἀγρυπνεῖν, νήφειν) in its consciousness of the time of the advent. The continuity of the Church and its ministry cannot therefore be interpreted simply in terms of historical succession on the stage of this world, or within the framework of secular history (the *schema* of this *aeon*), but must be interpreted in terms of the redemption of time in the Body of Christ. This Church redeems the time when it keeps awake, i.e. when it lives not by temporal succession, certainly not in bondage or subjection to it, but by finding its true being and real continuity in the new time of the resurrection. Thus the Church that has its mission within empirical history from age to age lives by the fact that succession on the plane of sinful history, 'as in Adam all die', has been emptied of meaning by participation in the risen humanity of Christ, 'so in Christ shall all be made alive' (1 Cor. 15.22). The Church that lives by historical succession and finds the guarantee of its life therein, seeks to live by the 'weak and beggarly elements' from which we have been redeemed (Gal. 4.9). Paul may plant and Apollos may water, but God gives the increase (1 Cor. 3.6).

(2) What the New Testament has to say about the redemption of the body is parallel to the redemption of time. Bodily structure as we know it in our world from day to day is bound up with creation and creation spoiled by man. It is structure that cannot be divorced from the history of mankind and

therefore from the sin of mankind. Indeed the whole of our creaturely world has become implicated in the fall of man and awaits the redemption of the body (Rom. 8.19f). All the structural forms or *schemata* of the cosmos belong to this passing age and are involved in the 'crumbling time' we have just been considering. But here the decay or corruption involved is interpreted in terms of hardening into rigidity (πώρωσις) which brings with it blindness and bondage to mankind. The outstanding example of that is recalcitrant Judaism. St. Paul has several ways of speaking about the death or decay of historical structure.

The principal way he has of speaking of this is in terms of law (*nomos*), for law is the form which this passing age assumes under the divine judgment and the means by which it seeks to entrench itself in finality. To men in their sin and estrangement the manifestation of the divine will becomes refracted in time and codified in rigid forms, while time takes on under guilt and judgment the character of fateful irreversibility. This means for man a very bitter bondage which St. Paul calls 'the curse of the law' (Gal. 3.10ff). It is from that that we are redeemed by Christ, and so St. Paul says: 'For I through the law am dead to the law that I might live unto God. I am crucified with Christ, nevertheless I live, yet not I, but Christ liveth in me: and the life which I now live in the flesh I live by the faith of the Son of God who loved me and gave himself for me' (Gal. 2.19f).

The Galatians, however, having begun their Christian life in grace, through the act of the Spirit, attempt to perfect it by walking (στοιχεῖν) according to the ordinances of this world (τὰ στοιχεῖα τοῦ κοσμοῦ), and so are dragged back again into the bondage of the law—the very law from which we are redeemed. 'When the fulness of time was come God sent forth his Son, made of a woman, made under the law, to redeem them that were under the law, that we might receive the adoption of sons. And because we are sons God has sent forth the Spirit of his Son into your hearts, crying, Abba, Father. Wherefore thou art no more a servant but a son, and if a son, then an heir of God through Christ' (Gal. 4.4f). Paul goes on to ask: 'How is it that, now after ye have known God, or rather are known of God, ye turn again to the weak and beggarly elements (στοιχεῖα) whereunto ye desire again to be in bondage? Ye observe days, months, and times, and years. I am afraid for you, lest I have bestowed upon you labour in vain. . . . My little children, I travail again in birth for you, until Christ be formed in you' (Gal. 4.9f, 19). Then Paul commands them to walk in the Spirit. 'If ye be led of the Spirit (πνεύματι ἄγεσθε), ye are not under the law. . . . If we live in the Spirit let us also walk in the Spirit (πνεύματι καὶ στοιχῶμεν)' (Gal. 5.18, 25). 'For in Christ the only thing that avails is a new creature (καινὴ κτίσις). And as many as walk according to this rule (τῷ κανόνι τούτῳ στοιχήσουσιν) peace be upon them, and mercy, and upon the Israel of God' (Gal. 6.15, 16).

In these passages Paul is using the term στοιχεῖν which means to go in a row in accordance with some principle of order, or to go in succession according to some principle of temporality.[1] By the noun (τὰ στοιχεῖα τοῦ κοσμοῦ) Paul refers to temporal successions or to temporal ordinances turned into dogmatic principles of the cosmos. Time is the underlying form of all structures, but as such time comes to assume certain immanent patterns in the cosmos which when erected into *nomos* are like the demonic ἐξουσίαι and ἄρχοντες which through *nomos* usurp the authority of God over man and seek to absolutise themselves. To walk according to temporal succession, or tradition, turned into a dogmatic principle (Col. 2.20; cf. Eph. 2.2) is not to walk according to Christ (Col. 2.8), for that is to subject oneself again to the tyrant forces from which we have been redeemed by the blood of Christ. Paul warns his converts therefore against the bondage of legal structures and temporal ordinances, and calls upon them to walk according to the Spirit (στοιχεῖν τῷ πνεύματι) for not law but Spirit is the time-form of the Church. This time-form is bound up with a new structure, the Spiritual Body of Christ. The legal structures or temporal ordinances drawn mainly from Judaism, with which the Galatians and Colossians sought to order and shape the Church, were 'a shadow of things to come, but the body is of Christ' (Col. 2.17). Here Paul is apparently using 'body' in a dual sense. On the one hand it means 'substance' or 'reality'

---

[1] For a fuller exposition see 'The Atonement and the Oneness of the Church', *S.J.T.*, 7, pp. 263f. See also the Dead Sea *Manual of Discipline* which uses similar language, 1.14f; 3.9ff; 4.16f; 9.12f. Cf. Josephus, *Wars of the Jews*, 2.8.7. A study of the tenets of the Essenes fully justifies Lightfoot's suggestion that it was against them that the Epistle to the Colossians was directed.

in contrast to mere shadows, but on the other hand it definitely refers to the Body of Christ as the context shows (Col. 2.9, 11, 19). The Church that is baptised with Christ's Baptism, or circumcised with His circumcision, has been delivered out of bondage to the legal structures of the cosmos and is dead to them, for it is concerned with a new life and a new pattern of life in the Body of the risen Christ (Col. 2.19f; 3.1f).

Here we proceed in time according to a new canon (τῷ κανόνι τούτῳ στοιχήσουσιν) which Paul describes in these terms. 'God forbid that I should glory, save in the cross of our Lord Jesus Christ, by whom the world is crucified unto me, and I unto the world. For in Christ Jesus neither circumcision availeth anything nor uncircumcision, but a new creature' (Gal. 6.14-16). By 'circumcision' Paul means literally Jewish circumcision, but also all that went along with it in the whole *nomos* of the Jewish tradition and succession (Gal. 5.3; Phil. 3.2f) and all the advantages that involved, 'the oracles' (Rom. 3.2), 'the adoption and the glory, and the covenants, and the giving of the law, and the service of God, and the promises and the fathers' (Rom. 9.4f). But to walk according to Christ (στοιχεῖν κατὰ Χριστόν) or to walk in the Spirit (στοιχεῖν πνεύματι) is not to walk according to these advantages regarded as *nomos* or *stoicheia*, and certainly not to boast in them. If boasting were required Paul had a great deal of which to boast. Who was more securely grounded than he in that 'advantage every way' (Rom. 3.1f) which the Jewish Church had? And so to the Philippians he cites his own perfection in the tradition of the Hebrews, its valid ordinances and their divine authorisation, but compared to Christ all that Paul calls 'flesh'. 'What things were gain to me, those I counted loss for Christ' (Phil. 3.7), and so he calls upon the Philippians to 'walk by the same rule' (τῷ αὐτῷ στοιχεῖν [κανόνι], Phil. 3.16), and thus to follow the Apostolic example (τύπον, Phil. 3.17).

Here we have a supreme lesson to learn from the Apostle who gave us the doctrine of the Church as the Body of Christ: that a church may be able to claim divine authorisation for its ordering, its appointments, and to boast of a valid succession or a historic episcopate, and yet all that is to be described as 'confidence in the flesh'. It will not do therefore to point to valid regulations and canonical traditions and to put them forward as claims and to stand on them as foundations, and certainly not to boast of them: for then they are simply to be regarded as στοιχεῖα τοῦ κόσμου.[1] The *canonical* way of living in the Body of Christ is to follow the Apostolic example of Paul and to walk by the same rule or canon as he: 'What things were gain to me, those I counted loss for Christ' (Phil. 3.7). 'God forbid that I should glory save in the cross of our Lord Jesus Christ, by whom the world is crucified unto me, and I unto the world. For in Christ Jesus what avails is a καινὴ κτίσις. As many as *proceed in time according to this rule* (ὅσοι τῷ κανόνι τούτῳ στοιχήσουσιν) peace be upon them, and mercy, and upon the Israel of God' (Gal. 6.14f).

To sum up our discussion so far: The Church on earth and in history is inescapably involved in space and time and in all the machinery of physical existence, and that involvement lies behind the significance of order. Its very bodily and historical existence requires structural and temporal order if it is to perform its mission in space and time. The form of this passing age, however, according to the New Testament, is the form of law or *nomos*, and the patterns of historical succession assume the character of cosmological principles or *stoicheia*, so that the Church in this age is inescapably involved in law and historical schematisation. But the real form and order of the Church are not to be looked for in terms of the laws and patterns of cosmic and temporal succession, but in Christ who died in sacrifice for us and who rose again, through whom the Church is crucified to the world and crucified to the law, that through the Spirit it might participate in the New Creation. All that lies behind the significance of order in the Church. And so, to turn to the language of the Epistle to the Romans, members of the Church are to present their bodies as a living sacrifice, holy and acceptable unto God which is their reasonable service, and *not to be schematised to this aeon*, but to be transformed by the renewing of their mind (Rom. 12.1f, the same argument as in Phil. 2.5f; 3.10f). It is on that basis that Paul goes on to speak of the membering of the One Body and the orders of the Church as deriving from the special gifts of the Spirit for the ministry of the Body (Rom. 12.4ff). The Church that is crucified with Christ belongs to the new divine order inaugurated by Christ's resurrection in Body. That Church is to be thought of as 'in

[1] Thus to walk κατὰ στοιχεῖα τοῦ κόσμου is the same as to walk κατὰ σάρκα (Rom. 8.4; 2 Cor. 10.2), and κατὰ τὸν αἰῶνα τοῦ κόσμου τούτου (Eph. 2.2).

the law to Christ' (ἔννομος Χριστοῦ, 1 Cor. 9.21) and as 'proceeding in the Spirit' (στοιχεῖν πνεύματι, Gal. 5.25). If therefore we are to have a doctrine of order, it must be the order of conformity to the death and resurrection of Christ, and orders are then to be thought of as the signs of the new divine order mediated to us through the death and resurrection of Christ, and signs that the new divine order is already breaking into the midst of the Church on earth and in history. That is why Paul speaks of orders in terms of the *charismata* of the Spirit.

It is apparent from all this that order in the Church is essentially ambiguous. The Church is inescapably involved in space and time and exercises its ministry within the limitations they impose on it. But the Church is wonderfully involved in the divine life of Christ and participates in the new age of the resurrection which has broken through the limitations of 'this evil aeon'. A true doctrine of order must do justice to both aspects of order and to both sides of the essential ambiguity. It must show that the Church, which continues to live in on-going history, lives as the Body of the risen and ascended Lord and therefore does not possess its orders in the unbroken continuum of the space and time of this world. How could it? It lives a life from beyond itself, and therefore looks beyond the historical forms of its orders to find its true being and form in the risen Humanity of Christ, and in the love that abides when all that is 'in part' shall be done away. This, however, does not mean the abrogation of the historical forms of order, any more than it means the abrogation of the Church's historical existence, but it does mean that they are relativised and that the Church is given a new orientation within them. The ascension means that the Church is sent to live its life and to exercise its ministry within the limitations of history, but here through the Spirit the limitations of history cease to be mere limitations for their finality is taken away; they now become doors or windows opening up toward the new divine order of the Church's life in Christ, signs pointing beyond themselves to the reality of the New Creation. But in so doing they themselves are transcended.

This does not mean that the Church must live and carry out its mission in history as *Ecclesia Triumphans*. Far from it, for that would be to seek to force the hand of the Coming King, and to live and work now as if the *parousia* had already taken place. That is, however, the temptation of every 'realised

56

eschatology' in its Roman or Protestant forms: to lose patience with the patience of Jesus (contrast Rev. 1.9). The Roman promulgation of the doctrine of the assumption of the Virgin Mary into heaven is the sign of incredible impatience, for it means a re-interpretation of the *parousia* of Christ in terms of the assumption of the Church.[1] What we human creatures think of as a 'coming down' is then but an upside down way of speaking of the exaltation of the Church into God![2] And so the Protestant counterpart to that is the programme of de-mythologising the ascension and *parousia* advocated by Rudolf Bultmann.

We are thrown back once again upon a serious doctrine of the resurrection and ascension of Christ. In the perspective of our discussion the resurrection means that the historical Jesus does not belong to crumbling time, to time that fades away like all history into vanity and dust, that the whole course of His obedience and His sacrifice on the Cross are not left to the corruption of a fallen world, to contingency and relativity, that all the earthly life and work of Jesus are not to be banished as possessing merely historical interest or to be forgotten as temporally irrelevant to our present actualities. The resurrection means that the historical Jesus is brought back out of the grave, out of the past because it is real historical happening which resists decay, because it is abiding reality that has penetrated through our mortal existence into eternal reality. 'I am he that liveth and was dead, and behold I am alive for ever more' (Rev. 1.18). He is 'the Lamb as it had been slain' (Rev. 5.6). The resurrection means that the crucified Jesus is actually risen from the dead, and has broken through the limitations of our corrupt existence into which He entered for our sakes, and in doing so has redeemed our humanity from vanity and our time from illusion, establishing Himself in the fulness of His Humanity and in the fulness of His time as the reality of our humanity and the reality of our time. This historical Jesus is no longer merely 'historical' in the sense that He belongs to history that irreversibly flows away into the past for ever, but within that history He is superior historical reality as actual and live happening in the continuous present. If

[1] See *S.J.T.*, 4, pp. 90-96.
[2] See additional note (2), p. 62.

Jesus had not risen in the same sphere of actuality in which He became incarnate, then we would yet be in our sins, for then His historical life and work, His atonement would all belong to crumbling time and vanity, and would be of no avail for us today. But the resurrection means that all that Jesus was for us and our salvation He is permanently and as such is present reality to us in the fulness of His historical humanity risen from the dead.

That is also the significance of the ascension. If Jesus Christ had not ascended and withdrawn Himself from the visible succession of history on the stage of this passing world, then we who live in passing time would be overwhelmed by the temptation to relegate the historical Jesus to the past and seek to have direct and immediate contact with Him as if He had not died for us on the Cross. The ascension means, therefore, that the risen Lord directs all our gaze back to the historical Jesus and forward to the coming Jesus. It directs all our gaze to the historical Jesus because it is on the ground of His Incarnation and the work of His Incarnation in atonement that the Risen Christ insists on making contact with us. The historical Jesus is the abiding *locus* for our meeting with the risen and ascended Lord—we make contact with Him only through His wounds (John 20.17ff). But we make contact with the historical Jesus as risen and ascended, not just as an object for historical investigation by the canons of credibility available for all other events in fading time, but as real historical happening in which the past is fully present reality. Through the ascension then Christ has withdrawn Himself from sight that we may find Him alive and risen in the historical Jesus as communicated through the Apostolic witness and tradition and through the Spirit be united to Him in His Humanity as the forgiven and redeemed.

The ascension directs our gaze also to the *parousia*. 'This same Jesus, which is taken up from you into heaven, shall so come in like manner as ye have seen him go unto heaven' (Acts 1.11).[1] 'This third dimension, the dimension indicated by the *parousia*, cannot be dropped from view, without endangering the dimensions of His present and His past. When it is dropped, the relation to Jesus will inevitably become a mere historical relation, His presence among His people will

---

[1] See the magnificent exposition of Barth in *Kirchliche Dogmatik*, 3/2: *Jesus, der Herr der Zeit*, pp. 524-616, and the review by F. W. Camfield, *S.J.T.*, 3, pp. 127ff.

be interpreted psychologically, and His being at the beginning of creation and in eternity will be regarded in the light of an overstress and exaggeration due to man's sense of the importance of the truths and values for which He stood. In Himself He will cease to be of cardinal importance.'[1]

It is in this time of the risen, ascended, and coming Jesus that the Church has its time, time for God and time for all men, time in the form of the Spirit in the midst of this passing age so that in the midst of passing time it is the time of meeting with Christ as His Body, and the time of the mission of Christ through His Body. It is the time of 'affliction and kingdom and patience' ($\acute{\upsilon}\pi o\mu o\nu\acute{\eta}$, Rev. 1.9) in which we are at once 'in the Spirit on the Lord's Day', and yet 'in the isle that is called Patmos' or wherever the Lord has placed us in His service (Rev. 1.9, 10).

The time of the ascension is thus of cardinal importance for a doctrine of the Church and its ministry. The ascension means the establishment of the Church in history with historical structure and form, in which the time of the Church is the time of faith, not yet the time of sight, the time when the realm of *grace* is not yet dissolved by the realm of *glory*. If Jesus during the three years of His earthly ministry had manifested His full divine glory so that men were confronted face to face with the ultimate Majesty of God, then they would have been planted at once in the *eschaton*, and historical time within which there is room for free meeting and decision would have been abrogated: the final judgment would have taken place. But the veiling of the glory which He had before the world was (John 17.1ff) meant that Jesus was giving men a chance to meet Him in free decision. He was holding them, so to speak, at arm's length away, revealing Himself to men in such a way as not to overwhelm and crush them, giving them time to repent, and room for decision. He came then veiling His glory, yet revealing Himself obliquely through parable and *kerygma* 'as they were able to hear' (Mark 4.33), giving enough light for them to believe, not enough to blind and judge them on the spot. That is why He always refused to give a compelling demonstration of Himself, even when He confronted men with the last things, for He came to evoke faith and love, to effect real meeting between God and man. Faith is not sight, but exists in that meeting

[1] F. W. Camfield, op. cit., p. 133.

between partial and final revelation (1 Cor. 13.7-13). Correlative to the earthly ministry of Jesus, the ascension means that Jesus has withdrawn Himself from history in order to allow the world time for repentance. He has not come to judge, but the Word which He speaks will be the judge at the last day (John 12.47f). He holds back His final unveiling in Majesty, holds back the final judgment when there will be no time to repent, and when, as the Apocalypse puts it, he that is filthy will be filthy still (Rev. 22.11). That is the time in which the Church exists and carries out its mission, within the succession of history where there is time between revelation and decision, time between decision and act, time between the present and the future. It is time where the present age is already interpenetrated by the age to come, but it is the time when the new age and all its final glory are held in eschatological reserve (κατέχειν), in order to leave room to preach the Gospel and give mankind opportunity to meet with God, to repent, and believe the Gospel.[1]

Within the succession of history and its structures and forms the Church is the sphere where through the Spirit the new world breaks into the old, the arena within the limitations of the old where God acts freely upon men through Word and Spirit and where men are summoned to response and obedience. If the Church were only a society within time, were but a social construct of historical succession, there would be no room for free meeting and decision, for everything would be determined by the processes of this world, the στοιχεῖα τοῦ κοσμοῦ. But the Church is the sphere where through the Cross of Christ the sovereign grace of God strikes into the heart of this world and draws all men into the sphere of His redeeming operation. In it men and women are delivered from the tyrant forces of bondage and are made free for God, so that real meeting in reconciliation and faith is effectually realised. The Church as the Body of Christ is the sphere within the time-form of this world where God and man meet in love and man is translated into the Kingdom of God's dear Son.

As such the Church does not live within the succession of history as a self-perpetuating institution, but as the *vis-à-vis* of

---

[1] This is the Biblical concept of μακροθυμία or ἀνοχή which belongs to the covenant mercies of God in OT and in NT. See Gen. 8.20ff; Exod. 34.6; Joel 2.13; Ps. 86.15; 103.8; 145.8; Rom. 2.4; 3.25; 9.22; 1 Tim. 1.16; 2 Pet. 3.9, 15.

the Kingdom of Christ, the covenant-partner of the ascended Lord, and carries out its ministry in holy counterpoint to the heavenly session at the right hand of God the Father Almighty. 'The Church is a function of the Kingdom, of the universal Lordship of God in Christ.'[1]

The ascension of Jesus Christ to the throne of God was the enthronement of the Word made flesh, the enthronement of the Lamb. It was the inauguration of His Kingdom in which 'God gave him to be the head over all things to the church, which is his body' (Eph. 1.22). But until the *parousia* He holds back the epiphany of Glory; He exercises His Kingdom only through His Priesthood, bestowing His Spirit upon the Church that the proclamation of the Word of the Cross may be power of God unto salvation to all who believe (1 Cor. 1.17ff). He waits to be gracious. And so the Church on earth lives and moves and has its being in the Kingdom and Patience of Jesus. As such the Church is given 'the keys of the Kingdom' (Matt. 16.19; cf. Luke 11.52; Rev. 1.18). 'Fear not little flock, for it is your Father's good pleasure to give you the kingdom' (Luke 12.32; cf. Luke 22.29f).[2] As Jesus breathed upon the disciples on Easter evening and said: 'Receive ye the Holy Spirit: whose soever sins ye remit, they are remitted unto them; and whose soever sins ye retain they are retained' (John 20.22f; cf. Matt. 16.19; Matt. 18.18), so He baptised the Church with His Spirit enduing it with power from on high (Acts 1.5-8; Luke 24.49) thus giving it to participate in the Kingdom of Christ. But this participation of the Church in the Kingdom is only through its priesthood, its ministry as suffering servant: 'in *affliction*, and in the Kingdom and patience of Jesus' (Rev. 1.9). 'If we suffer, we shall also reign with him' (2 Tim. 2.12). The Church overcomes by the blood of the Lamb (John 16.33) and the Word of its testimony (Rev. 12.11).

It is as suffering servant that the Church in history is the covenant-partner of the Royal Priest above, and reigns with Him as it carries the Cross, proclaiming the Word of the Gospel and dispensing the mysteries of God. In ascension Christ has

---

[1] J. A. T. Robinson, *The Historic Episcopate* (edited by K. Carey), p. 15.

[2] Does the συναλιζόμενος of Acts 1.4, a *hapaxlegomenon* in the NT, indicate that Christ established a covenant of salt between Himself and the Church, gathering up and fulfilling the covenant of salt established with the Aaronic Priesthood (Num. 18.19) and the covenant of salt established with the Davidic Kingdom (2 Chron. 13.5)? At any rate the Church is a Royal Priesthood (1 Pet. 2.9).

left the Church with the Word and Sacraments and it is in its ministry of Word and Sacraments that it is maintained as Body of the ascended Head, formed into His image and ordered as the instrument of His Kingdom.

[1] I am aware that in recent years many Roman Catholic theologians have been trying to re-interpret the notion of *corpus mysticum* with the aid of a Christology in which greater justice is given to the historical humanity of Christ, but how far they are from succeeding is apparent in the papal encyclical *Mystici Corporis Christi* of June 29, 1943. The encyclical rightly rejects a separation between the Church mystical and the Church juridical, but when it goes on to identify outright the mystery of the Church with the ecclesiastical institution, it provides a signal illustration of the dialectic noted above. Just as in the field of Christology ebionitism and docetism, opposite to one another as they are, always tend to pass into one another, so in the field of Roman ecclesiology we find a similar process going on. In the last resort however the monophysitism that lurks in Roman Christology and Mariology, and the docetism in its doctrine of transubstantiation, determine the ultimate nature of its ecclesiology. The hunger for the humanity of Christ in the Roman Church is just as apparent in its Mariology as in movements like the cult of the Heart of Jesus.

[2] This is quite consonant with the teaching of those Roman theologians who hold that the assumption of Mary is an eschatological image of the assumption of the Church which will take place at the *parousia*, for what will take place *manifestly* at the *parousia* is not in principle different from what takes place *sacramentally* in the Eucharistic *parousia*. In the last resort it is the identity of the Kingdom with the visible Church on earth, and the doctrine of transubstantiation in the Mass, which determine the Roman understanding of the transmutation of the earthly into a heavenly reality in the consummation. Cf. Thomas Aquinas, *Summ. Theol. Suppl.* q. 91. art. 4 et 5, and *Scriptum s. Sent.* IV. dist. 48. q. 11, art. 1 et seq. for an account of the final transmutation.

IV

THE PRIESTHOOD OF THE CHURCH

THE Church has been incorporated through the Word and Baptism into Christ so as to become His Body. This takes place within the time of the patience of Jesus between His ascension and His *parousia*, and within that time the Church is ever being renewed as the Body of Christ through the ministry of the Word and through communion in the Blood and the Body of Christ. Thus the Word and Sacraments in their inseparable unity span the whole life and mission of the Church in the last times inaugurated by Pentecost, holding together the First Coming with the Final Coming in the one *parousia* of Him who was, who is, and who is to come. It is therefore in terms of the Word and Sacraments that we are to articulate our understanding of the ministry of the Church, of its order and of the nature of its priesthood functioning through that order. An examination of the Biblical witness at this point makes it clear that the order of the Church is determined by the real presence of the Son of Man in Word and Sacrament, and that the priesthood of the Church, while distinct from the unique vicarious Priesthood of Christ, is nevertheless determined by the form of His Servant-existence on earth.

We cannot do better than begin by looking at the teaching of St. Paul in 1 Corinthians 10-14 particularly.[1]

Shocking disorder had broken out in the Church at Corinth which had even manifested itself in schism at the Lord's Table breaking up its corporate nature and turning the κυριακὸν δεῖπνον into an ἴδιον δεῖπνον. From the disorder at the Eucharist the whole church was affected in a disorderly way of life. To counter that deteriorating situation the Apostle wrote this Epistle designed to be read at the celebration of the Eucharist as *kerygma* 'in demonstration of the Spirit and of power' (1 Cor. 2.4; cf. 1.17ff), to reimpose truth upon error

[1] Cf. the treatment of this by E. Käsemann in *Evangelische Theologie* 1948, 9/10, and by H. Doebert in *Evangelische Theologie*, 1949, 11.

63

and order upon disorder. It was Apostolic Word sent to order the sacramental life of the Church and to bring it back into conformity to the love of Christ that it might be built up in love as His one undivided Body. The all-important fact here is the Apostolic Word, the Word of God mediated through the Apostolic tradition (1 Cor. 15.3ff) which forms the Church and shapes the *Agape*-Eucharist, so that the Church in Corinth through Baptism and Communion may indeed be the Body of the risen Christ (1 Cor. 15.12ff).

St. Paul reminds the Corinthians of the Church of the Old Testament and what happened to it τυπικῶς, for 'they were written for our admonition upon whom the ends of the world are come' (εἰς οὓς τὰ τέλη τῶν αἰώνων κατήντηκεν). As elsewhere, so here St. Paul uses the same language for the Sacraments of the Old Testament and for the Sacraments of the New Testament.[1] All the Israelites were baptised in the cloud and in the sea, that is by Spirit and water, and they all partook of the same spiritual food and drink (1 Cor. 10.2f), but that did not give them any security apart from obedience to God's Word. Participation in the Sacraments is not in itself a guarantee of salvation, for along with sacramental communion there must go the whole building up and ordering of the Body in the love of Christ. When the Sacraments are taken in conjunction with the bodily obedience they involve, they reveal the true form and order of the Church.

By Baptism we are incorporated into One Body but that unity is preserved (1 Cor. 10.16f; 12.12f) and made visible in the Lord's Supper (1 Cor. 11.18ff). Here the whole life and form of the Church's life are seen to derive from a source beyond the Church, in the Blood and Body of Christ, and can only be maintained by continual return to that source. At the same time it is made clear that as communion in the Blood of Christ and communion in His Body belong inseparably together (1 Cor. 10.16f), so the compacting of the Church into one ordered Body of love in Christ reposes upon atonement through His Blood.[2]

St. Paul then develops his argument in four stages as it arises out of the baptismal and eucharistic κοινωνία.

[1] Thus Circumcision and Passover are used to describe Baptism and the Lord's Supper (Col. 2.11; 1 Cor. 5.7; 2 Cor. 1.20); so here Baptism and the Lord's Supper are ascribed to the Church in the Old Testament (1 Cor. 10.2f).

[2] Cf. 'The Atonement and the Oneness of the Church', *S.J.T.*, 7/3, pp. 245ff.

(1) In the eleventh and twelfth chapters he speaks of the ordering of the Church as it comes together to celebrate the Lord's Supper. This takes place in the orderly *paradosis* of the Apostolic Church (1 Cor. 11.23) and is a renewing of the Covenant founded in the Blood of Christ and therefore a pledging of the Church to live and work as a covenant-partner of Christ,[1] that is, as His Body, which must be consciously discerned in and through the participation (1 Cor. 11.24ff). In the ordering of the Eucharist, and for the Church at the Eucharist, special χαρίσματα or gifts are given. It is made clear in the twelfth chapter that the Lord's Supper and the χαρίσματα belong inseparably together, and that the charismatic gifts are to be used in accordance with the promulgation of God's will in the New Covenant or Testament. This is the *New* Covenant (Jer. 31.31f) and involves a *new* creation, for in and through the sacramental participation the *new* divine order in the risen Body of Christ is made manifest.[2] To the nature of that new divine order Paul returns in the fifteenth chapter when he discusses the resurrection of Christ in the same sphere of actuality in which we are. This new order of the Church is given in and through the Lord's Supper, as it is celebrated in obedience to the divine ordinance.

(2) In the thirteenth chapter St. Paul goes on to describe the nature of the new divine order as Love or *Agape*. That divine Love is manifest in the ordering of the Supper in the midst of a love-feast or *Agape* and in the mutual service the charismatic gifts involve. Behind and beyond the rites and the gifts there breaks in God's love which is to be lived out in the power of the One Spirit. All the historical patterns of the Church's life will pass away but love will not pass away. That love is already given to the Church in its communion with Christ and as such its manifestation in the ordering of the Church on earth is an expression of the coming Kingdom when we shall see face to face and know as we are known (1 Cor.

---

[1] Cf. here the Words of the Lord as recorded in the Lukan account, in which He speaks of the ordering of the Disciples and the Church at the Supper: 'I appoint unto you a kingdom as my Father hath appointed unto me (κἀγὼ διατίθεμαι ὑμῖν καθὼς διέθετό μοι ὁ πατήρ μου βασιλείαν) that ye may eat and drink at my table in my kingdom and sit on thrones judging the twelve tribes of Israel' (Luke 22.30). That is the ordering of the Church into a Royal Priesthood at and through the Lord's Supper. Cf. Acts 1.4; Rev. 1.5f; 1 Pet. 2.2ff.

[2] Cf. Matt. 26.29: 'I will not drink henceforth of this fruit of the vine, until that day when I drink it *new* with you in my Father's kingdom.'

13.10f). In the words of another Epistle it is 'love which is the bond of perfection' (ἡ ἀγάπη, ὅ ἐστιν σύνδεσμος τῆς τελειότητος, Col. 3.14). That love is the very *esse* of the Church given to it through union with Christ, and manifests itself in the Church in the form of self-denial, suffering and service (1 Cor. 13.3ff). This love which is given to the Church in history in χαρίσματα and operates through διακονία, reaches out to the divine τέλος of the eternal Kingdom (1 Cor. 15.28, etc.).

(3) This being so, in the visible ordering of the Church, everything must be made to serve the real form and nature of the Church in love. And so in the fourteenth chapter St. Paul goes on to show how the charismatic ordering of the eucharistic fellowship is to be undertaken in accordance with love. Everything turns upon the building up of the Church in love as the Body of Christ. The Church which has communicated in the Body and Blood of Christ is committed in its whole life in the body to bodily obedience in love, but that is to be expressed in the ordering of the Church within its own membership. Earlier in the Epistle Paul had spoken of the Church as 'God's building' (1 Cor. 3.9), as 'the Temple of God' indwelt by the Spirit (1 Cor. 3.16f). As a wise masterbuilder Paul had laid the foundation in Christ, but he commands the Corinthians to take heed how they build on that foundation, for everything will be put to the test by fire of God to discover the work that really 'abides' (1 Cor. 3.10f). In 1 Corinthians thirteen Paul has made it indubitably clear that the things that abide are faith, hope, and love, and the greatest of these is love (1 Cor. 13.13). Everything in the Temple of God and its upbuilding must be directed toward that end. All the *charismata* will pass away and with them all the offices of the ministry, the Sacraments and even faith and hope, but love endures on into eternity as the abiding reality.

It belongs to the nature of the case that order in the Church which is the expression here and now of the coming Kingdom and is of the nature of the divine love, is not to be possessed, or is to be possessed only as the Spirit is possessed. The nature of the *charismata* is determined by the Spirit who is Himself both the *Giver* and the *Gift*, so that even as Gift He remains transcendent to the Church, 'the Lord the Spirit' (2 Cor. 3.17— which determines the nature of the ministry described in 2 Cor. 4.1ff). Though in the gift of the Spirit diversities of gifts are bestowed which are distinct from the Spirit, they all repose upon the One Spirit and are determined by the nature of His Presence, or of the real presence of Christ through the Spirit.

In working this out for the Church at Corinth St. Paul is concerned to warn them against two dangers, legalism and anarchy. (a) Participation in the ordinances of the Lord does not grant the Church legal security. The Church is to walk not according to law but according to the Spirit, and as the Church through the communion of the Spirit participates in the Body of Christ it is given real determination of form and order. But everything must be subordinate to love, in which each serves the other and is subject to the other. It is thus that the divine order supervenes upon the Church forming it into the image of Christ and building it up as His Body. (b) On the other hand this mutual ordering of the Church in love means self-denial and restraint upon the part of the Church and its members so that 'all may learn and all be comforted' (1 Cor. 14.31). 'The spirits of the prophets are subject to the prophets, for God is not the author of confusion but of peace as in all the churches of the saints' (1 Cor. 14.32f). St. Paul does not say that the Spirit is subject to the prophet but that the gifts of the Spirit are to be used in such a way that 'all things are to be done decently and in order' (πάντα δὲ εὐσχημόνως καὶ κατὰ τάξιν γινέσθω 1 Cor. 14.40). The Spirit can no more be managed than the real Presence of Christ, but the spirits of the prophets as they are moved charismatically by the Holy Spirit are to be subject to the service of love. Thus there must be definite order in the eucharistic fellowship, but such order in which the Church serves Christ, is obedient to the Spirit, and engages in the mutual edification of love.

(4) The purpose of this order is to make room in the midst for the presence of the risen Christ so that the Church's fellowship becomes the sphere where the resurrection of Christ is effectively operative here and now. In the resurrection each will rise in his own order (ἕκαστος δὲ ἐν τῷ ἰδίῳ τάγματι, 1 Cor. 15.23) but that has already begun in the Church on earth which through the Spirit is already one Body with Christ. Thus the whole ordering of the Church on earth must be poised upon its expectation of the resurrection in body, and must therefore be an ordering of the Church as *soma pneumatikon* according to its real nature as disclosed in the resurrection of

Christ from the dead. Order in the Church, deriving from the eucharistic fellowship in which we 'proclaim the Lord's death till he come' (1 Cor. 11.26) takes on an essentially eschatological character. Apart from that eschatological perspective, order is dead for it does not serve the resurrection, and does not manifest either the love of Christ or His coming again to reign. And so St. Paul draws the Epistle to its close with the words: 'If any man love not the Lord Jesus Christ, let him be anathema: *Maran atha*' (1 Cor. 16.22).

We must now proceed to discuss more fully the relation of order to the *parousia* of Christ in Word and Sacrament, and the nature of the Church's ministry thus ordered.

(1) The Apostolic ordering of the eucharistic fellowship in Corinth demands of us a consideration of the other and secondary sense of Apostolic succession: the continuation of the Church in the Apostolic tradition of Word and Sacrament. 'Be ye followers of me even as I am of Christ' (1 Cor. 11.1; 4.16; 1 Thess. 1.6; Phil. 3.17). In this sense we may legitimately speak of an Apostolic succession in history. The Church continues to be Apostolic when, resting upon the Apostolic foundation and determined by the unfolding of the Mind of Christ within the Apostolic tradition, i.e. the New Testament, it continues throughout history to conform to the Apostolic doctrine.

In the most concrete sense this means a succession of obedience to the Holy Scriptures as the source and norm of the Church's continued existence. The Apostolic Church is the Church that lives by the New Testament as its *canon* of life and faith (cf. above on Gal. 6.16 and Phil. 3.16). This Church continues to be begotten from age to age in the Apostolic tradition on the ground of exegetical study of Holy Scripture and as it is edified by its teaching. It is thus that the Apostolic Word gives the Church its form and shapes and orders it upon the foundation of the Apostles (1 Cor. 3.9ff). By listening to the Apostolic witness, by the obedience of faith to Christ's revelation through the Apostles, the Church continues to be formed anew in the image of Christ, and so lives throughout the changes of history and throughout all temporal succession in such a way as not to be conformed to this world but to be transformed by the renewing of its mind. Apostolic Scripture becomes also the criterion and creative norm of the Church's catholicity. The Church that fails to be ordered by the truth of the Apostolic Scriptures, which refuses to be re-formed and cleansed and purged by the Word of Truth, calls in question its own apostolicity and so its catholicity, for it detaches itself from the foundation of the Church that has been laid in Christ. The apostolically ordered Church is the Church which throughout all the changes of history continues to be identical with itself in its foundation, and does not alter its nature by changing that foundation or deform itself by building upon that foundation wood, hay, stubble which will not stand the test of the divine judgment (1 Cor. 3.12f; Heb. 12.25-29). The Church has not only been rooted and grounded in Christ through the Apostolic *kerygma* and *paradosis* but continues to be built up in the Body of Christ as an ordered succession in obedience, in faith, in doctrine, in service.

This succession in obedience to the Word is inseparable from succession in being. Because in the Incarnation revelation and reconciliation are one in the unity of Word and Deed in Christ, continuity in the Apostolic Church is succession in the unity of knowing and being, of word and deed, of message and ministry. The living Body apostolically begotten through the incorruptible Word continues in being in history. As such it is the continuation, certainly not of Christ nor of the Incarnation, but of the Church which ever becomes the Body of Christ through Word and Sacrament.

We may put this otherwise. In the Incarnation God's Word has indissolubly bound itself to a human and historical form in Jesus Christ, such that there is no Word of God for us apart from actual event in our world. The Church of this Word become flesh, the Church as the Body of the Incarnate Son, involves in its very existence and structure the time-relations that are involved by the Word in the historical Jesus. To cut the link between the Church and the historical particularity of the Incarnation is to transubstantiate the Church into some docetic and timeless *corpus mysticum*, and to sever the Church from any saving act of God in our actual flesh and blood historical existence. And so we must say that although the Word assumed a unique form in history in the Incarnate Son, the Word about this Son which through the Spirit is the Word of the Son, assumes still a temporal and worldly form in the Church, begetting the Church in the course of history as the

Body of Christ. As the Word of God became irrevocably involved in a physical event, so in the Church the Word of God in the Apostolic witness is involved in a physical event and meets us in the sphere of creaturely reality to which we belong. In other words, God through the Incarnation and the Apostolic witness has ordained that we receive His Word through the historical communication of other men, so that the communication of the Word and the growth of the Church as historical community are correlative. Here it is the Apostolic tradition of the Holy Sacraments that enshrines the continuity of the Church's being in history, as St. Paul says: 'I have received of the Lord that which by tradition I delivered unto you' (ἐγὼ παρέλαβον ἀπὸ τοῦ κυρίου, ὃ καὶ παρέδωκα ὑμῖν, 1 Cor. 11.23), and he is speaking of the *traditio corporis* in the Lord's Supper which is the creative centre of the Church's continuity as Body of Christ.

That is the Apostolic succession in the secondary sense, for it is through the Apostolic foundation that the corporeality of the Word is extended and mediated to a corporeal world by such physical, historical events as the Bible, Preaching, Sacraments, the physical society of the members of the Church, the historical communication and edification, and all that that entails from age to age. As this historical actuality and concrete community built on the foundation of the Apostles, the Church is the Temple of God on earth. This stark actuality and corporeality of the Church is very clearly put by St. Paul in the sixth chapter of First Corinthians where he is insisting that the Christian life has to be lived out in the actual bodies of Christians. 'The body is for the Lord and the Lord for the body' (1 Cor. 6.13). 'Know ye not that your bodies are the members of Christ. . . . Know ye not that your body is the temple of the Holy Spirit who is within you?' (1 Cor. 6.15, 19). It is not surprising therefore to find Paul speaking of spiritual or rational worship (λογικὴ λατρεία) as the living sacrifice of our actual bodies (σώματα, Rom. 12.1). The continuity of the Church is a *somatic* continuity, and its order within that continuity is of a *somatic* kind.

It is this mutual involution of the *somatic* with the spiritual, of the Body of Christ with the Mind of Christ, that is so strongly emphasised in the New Testament doctrine of the Church and its function. It is not only persons that are members of Christ, but their bodies, so that to make their bodies the members of a harlot is an unmentionable *horrendum* (1 Cor. 6.15), to circumcise the body with a view to fulfilling the law or to glorifying in the flesh is to put off Christ and to make Him of none effect (Gal. 5.2f; 6.12f; cf. Col. 2.11f), and to baptise people twice is to crucify Christ all over again (Heb. 6.4f). Thus the bodily form of the Church and the spiritual, the outer historical form and the inner dogmatic form, are quite inseparable.

It is for that very reason that the corporeal nature of the Church as shaped by the Word of the Gospel and informed by the Spirit in the power of the resurrection means the breaking up and the relativising of the historical forms of the Church throughout its mission. The Church is sent out into history and is made under the law as servant of Christ within the form and fashion of history under judgment, but in the nature of the case the very fact that the Church is joined in One Body and One Spirit with Christ risen from the dead means that the Church is sent not to be fettered by the limitations and patterns of history but to use them for the work of proclaiming the Word of God. Indeed only as these limitations and patterns are broken through in their using can the Church be ordered as the Body of Christ. As through the fraction of the bread the Church ever becomes one Body in the Lord's Supper, so the Church that dares to proclaim that death till He come and to enact that proclamation in the mortification of its members on earth, finds itself ordered according to the new humanity after the image of the Creator.

It is thus in the Sacrament of the Lord's Supper above all that the two aspects of order are held together, the aspect that derives from the *nomos*-form of historical succession on the stage of this world, and the aspect that derives from the new being of the Church in the risen Lord. As we have already seen from St. Paul's Word to the Corinthian Church, we have to think this out in terms of the *charismata* and their relation to the real presence of Christ. They are the means by which the ascended Christ who sends down His Spirit upon the Church orders it in the love of God. Thus the *charismata* have validation only in real presence of Christ to the Church.

That is not to deny tradition or even juridical succession, but to subordinate them to the presence of the living Lord, and to give outward successions in ministerial orders their place as signs of *charismata* in the Church, as signs of the divine New Order which in the Gospel and Sacraments is ever breaking through the Church into the world and ever being realised afresh in our midst. At the root this involves quite a different notion of validity of orders. It is the duty of orders to serve the living Christ, to open up the Church and make room for the risen presence of Christ, the Church's Lord, whereas orders, regarded as a closed succession, really mean the death of Church order. In other words, in the Church as the Body of Christ, we must have such orders as do not by-pass the resurrection of Jesus Christ, and such a view of the true form of the Church that the living Christ today is not bound by the forms and ordinances which He is pleased to use from age to age.

That is most apparent in the Eucharistic communion of the Church where Church order is seen to be only *in actu*. At the Eucharist Christ is fully present, present bodily, and it is there that in the profoundest sense the Church becomes the Church as Body of Christ. With the Body of Christ the form of that Body is given and maintained. Church order is this form of the Body, and orders belong therefore to the form of the Church given to it as it engages in the communion of the Body and Blood of Christ, as it carries out the ordinance of the Lord, the Head of the Body. Thus in the Eucharist the Church assumes true form and order in obedience to the Word, but as such that order is not static, but dynamic, not a state but action. It cannot be abstracted from the Real Presence of the Risen Lord and then used as a criterion to judge the Church or to establish the validity of its ministry.[1] That would be the essence of self-justification.

If Church order is taken from the Eucharist, however, we have to remember that Christ gives Himself and reveals Himself to us in it only in part, for He is veiled behind the elements as well as revealed through them. That is, as we have seen, the importance of the doctrine of the ascension. We do not see Christ now, do not discern His Body, in the same way that we shall do at His coming again. That means that the whole

[1] 'To establish the validity of the ministry on grounds independent of the authority of the living Church (e.g. by linear succession of episcopal consecration), and then to judge whether a church is part of the Body by whether it has a valid ministry, is to invert the whole New Testament conception.' J. A. T. Robinson, *The Historic Episcopate* (edited by K. Carey), p. 15.

question of Church order is no magnitude such that we can exercise control over it. By the ascension it is withdrawn from the arena of our disposal. Because it belongs to the nature of Revelation that it assumes concrete worldliness as human word, human form, and human ordinance, the Church will manifest in definite orders the true form of the Body of Christ in its order, but on the other hand, because this true form is bound up with Revelation the Church will never be able to transcribe or materialise that form in the worldly conditions of time and history in any perfect or indelible way. A direct reading off of Church order from the Lord's Supper is therefore impossible on this side of the *parousia*. Because Revelation meets us in the creaturely reality of our fallen world, it conceals Christ behind Proclamation and Sacrament as well as reveals Him. It is of the nature of mystery manifest in the flesh (1 Tim. 3.16; cf. 3.9; Eph. 1.9; 3.3f; 6.19; Col. 1.26f; 2.2; 4.3, etc.). This means that we cannot set Church order, which partakes of that mystery in the midst of its worldliness, side by side with worldly order and give it the same sort of visibility, ascribe to it the same sort of validity, or think that in any way we can hold it down and use it in the same manner. So long as we wait for the redemption of the body, therefore, we are forbidden to have a static condition in the Church as if we already possessed fully valid orders or possessed them otherwise than in the mystery of a worldliness that is already under judgment. Real order in the Church is only visible in orders that serve it truly, acknowledging its dimension in depth in the ascension of Christ, and never in orders that seek to control it.[1]

(2) We have now to examine the nature of the priesthood that is revealed in the Word and Sacraments.

According to the *Catechismus Romanus* of 1566 (2.7.23)[2] there

---

[1] This has been well put by W. H. Vanstone in *The Historic Episcopate* (edited by K. Carey), p. 40. 'The New Testament does not point to the idea of a Spirit-bearing structure. The Spirit is not bound; and therefore we must reject, on the one hand, discussion of ecclesiastical structure in terms of validity: we must reject the theory of a single, determinate structure as decisive for the presence of the Spirit and the being of the Church. We must reject, on the other hand, discussion of ecclesiastical structure in terms of utility; we must reject the theory of a comparative evaluation of various structural forms in terms of their effectiveness in mediating the fruits of the Spirit. *We are led by the New Testament to discuss the problem of structure in terms neither of validity nor of utility, but of meaning.* The structure of the Church is not the medium but the expression of the Spirit. Thus the measure of the fullness of the Church is the degree to which it bears witness, in its structural being, to the nature and meaning of God's act of redemption.'

[2] See the excellent discussion by M. Schmaus, *Katholische Dogmatik* 4/1, pp. 130ff.

is a twofold priesthood in the Church, one which it calls *interius* and the other *externum*, a distinction which reposes upon the distinction between the Sacraments of Baptism and Eucharist.

Baptism, not confirmation, as Professor Schmaus has pointed out,[1] is the Sacrament of the general or corporate priesthood of the Church, for it is through Baptism that we are incorporated into the Body of Christ and are inserted into the ministry of His Body. All who are baptised into Christ are baptised into the Royal Priesthood, so that it is baptismal incorporation that gives us the rock foundation for a doctrine of order.

In the Lord's Supper, however, there takes place a special qualification or modification of priesthood which arises out of its very celebration in decency and in order: and that ordering of the Church fellowship at the Table, as we have seen, is revealed and governed by the distribution of diverse *charismata*. These diverse gifts are harmonised in a fellowship where proclamation of the Word or prophesying with interpretation gives articulation to the whole. This is the essential ministry of the Word, the most important of all the *charismata* (1 Cor. 14.1f; Acts 6.2f, etc.),[2] so that without it there can be no edifying service in the Church (1 Cor. 14.1ff).

It is at this point that the churches which seek to be obedient to the New Testament have so strong a controversy with the Roman Church because it has relativised the place which the priesthood of the Word occupies in the Christian Church, and has allowed a situation to arise which is remarkably parallel to that which the great prophets of the Old Testament found and sought to redress in Israel. That situation was brought to its climax in the crucifixion, as we have seen. It was essentially the same question which was at stake in the Reformation.

The Sacraments are above all the Sacraments of the Word made flesh, and so they are called Sacraments of the Gospel. As such by their very nature they can only be two in number, Baptism which is the Sacrament of once and for all incorporation into Christ, and the Eucharist which is the Sacrament of

[1] Op. cit., p. 133f.
[2] Under the ministry of the Word Paul includes Apostles, Evangelists, Prophets, Teachers. They differ rather much, for the Apostle has a unique relation to the Revelation and Tradition of the Word, but even the Apostle's main function is the ministry of the Word in contrast to the Sacraments: Acts 6.2ff; 1 Cor. 1.17f.

continued renewal in that incorporation. But both are strictly speaking two 'moments' of the one Mystery, 'God manifest in the flesh' (1 Tim. 3.9), 'Christ in you the hope of glory' (Col. 1.27), *the mystery of the fulfilled Word* (Col. 1.24f) in the Church which is Christ's Body, and so it is the mystery of union between Christ and His Church (Eph. 5.32). It is the Word of God which gives the Sacraments their unity, and their reality, though the Sacraments are the differing forms of the Word become visible and bodily event in the midst of the Church. Because the Sacraments are Sacraments of the Word made flesh, they are nothing apart from the Word, and so Augustine used to insist so strongly that it is the Word which sacramentalises the ordinance and turns it into a Sacrament: *Accedat verbum ad elementum et fiet sacramentum* (*Homil. in Joann.* 80.3). But the Sacraments are given in order that what the Spirit does through the Word in begetting the Church as the Body of Christ may become actual event in our flesh and blood, so that we in our mortal bodies may bear about the dying of the Lord Jesus Christ that His life also may be made manifest in our mortal flesh. That is the end of the ministry of the Word (2 Cor. 4.1ff).

We do not get the proper perspective until we see with the Fourth Gospel that the flesh of Jesus Christ did what was divine not in virtue of its own activity but in virtue of the Word united with it. Thus in and through the Word we feed upon the flesh and drink the blood of Christ (John 6.51ff). The Word is itself the all-inclusive Sacrament of the Word made flesh which through the Spirit begets the Church as Body in sacramental union with Christ. It is because the Word is given this nature that through the Spirit it sacramentalises the Sacraments. 'It is the Spirit that quickeneth; the flesh profiteth nothing: the words that I speak unto you, they are Spirit and they are life' (John 6.63). And so at the Last Supper Jesus said to the Disciples: 'Now ye are clean through the *word* which I have spoken unto you' (John 15.2). 'If a man love me, he will keep my *word*: and my Father will love him, and we will come unto him, and make our abode with him' (John 14.23). It is thus through the Word that Christ comes to cleanse, to abide in us, to feed us upon His flesh and blood, so that we may abide in Him as the branches abide in the Vine (John 15.1ff). That is to say, it is through the Word of Christ that we are incorporated into Him and become His Body.

It is because Christ comes to us as the Word and gives us His real presence through the Word and so unites us to Himself that Word and Sacrament belong inseparably together. Both lose their significance and efficacy when separated, for the relation of Word to Sacrament is to be understood in terms of the relation between the Head of the Body to the members of the Body. As it is the Head which governs and orders the members, so it is the transcendent Word which governs and orders the Sacraments. Thus in and through and over the Sacraments the ordering power comes from the real Presence of Christ the Head of the Body addressing the Church, summoning it to obedience and love, governing it through His Word, and fashioning it to be His Body.

In that, as we have seen, the Apostles occupied a unique position as the foundation of the Church, for it was through them that the Mind of Christ came to be articulated in the Church as divine Word in human form and yet prior to, and transcendent to, the Church. Hence the Apostles always come first in the Pauline lists of the *charismata* (Eph. 4.11; 1 Cor. 12.29, etc.). But within the Church the ministry of the Word, through evangelists who establish congregations or through prophets and teachers who build them up in the faith, occupies the primary place, for it is the ministry of Word that continues to beget and maintain the Church, and it is the proclamation of the Word to the Church which effectively forms it as the Body of Christ and preserves it as Body from usurping the place and authority of the Head.

This Word proclaimed as divine event becomes event in the bodily existence of the Church and is fulfilled as Word in the sacramental ordinances given by Christ for this very purpose. Thus the Word as the ordering element in the life of the Church, actually fulfils its ordination in the celebration of the Sacraments. In other words, it is as the Word becomes event in the sacramental ordinances that the Church as Body takes shape and form under the ordering of the Word of the ascended Head. As such the Sacraments mean the enactment of the authority of Christ over the Church and its life and ministry, and so the ministry of the Word and Sacraments involves a *charisma* of oversight (ἐπισκοπή) over the whole congregation and its worship, in which the unity of Word and Sacrament, and the proper relation of Sacrament to the Word may be maintained in the Church which is the Body united to Christ as its Head. Thus an *episcopos* presides over the fellowship of the Church by exercising the ministry of Word and Sacrament, but in such a manner that he is to be accounted a *steward* (οἰκονόμος) of the mysteries of God and an able minister (ὑπηρέτης) of the Spirit (1 Cor. 4.1f; cf. 2 Cor. 4.1ff). It is above all at the eucharistic fellowship that this is revealed and actually takes shape, for it is there that the corporate priesthood of the whole Body, answering through obedience to the Word of the ascended Priest receives a qualification and ordering which gives rise to the *charisma* of the presbyter-bishop. It is in the eucharistic fellowship that the whole interrelation of the members of the Body in subordination to the Head reaches its fullest expression so that it is in terms of the Eucharist and through the Eucharist that the Word orders the ministry of the Church.

It was for this reason that the great theologians of the thirteenth century (in agreement with Peter Lombard, *Sent. IV. dist.* 24), Albert the Great, Bonaventura, and Thomas Aquinas, all insisted that 'the Sacrament of Order is ordained in order to the Eucharist, which is the Sacrament of Sacraments' (cf. Aquinas, *Summ. Theol. Suppl.* q. 27.4.2-3).[1] That is to say, while the order of the priesthood or presbyterate is ordained to celebrate the Eucharist within the corporate priesthood of the whole Body, the order of priesthood is itself ordered by the Sacrament of the Eucharist. That is why the same theologians insisted that the episcopate, as distinct from the presbyterate, is not properly speaking an *order* and does not belong therefore

[1] Our difference with them, of course, lies in the place accorded to the Word in the Sacraments. When the Word is not given the dominant place, two things appear to happen: (1) The unity of Baptism and Eucharist as Sacraments of the Word made flesh is broken up, and they are then ordered together within a hierarchy or graduation of sacramental ordinances, the so-called seven Sacraments, and the Sacrament of Order is also graduated into seven orders. Throughout here the integrating element is not the ministry of the Word but jurisdiction, which tends to alter the whole notion of the episcopate. (2) The understanding of grace primarily as the relation of the divine Being as Cause to a divine creaturely being as the operation, rather than in terms of Word and Spirit, gives rise to a philosophical conception of theology articulated in *Summae*. In contrast, Reformed theology concerned with the Word of God, proclamation of it, and obedient conformity to it in the life of the Church, articulates theology in *Dogmatics*. The fact that Roman theology has been moving away from *Summae* to *Dogmatics*, which brings the teaching of the Church to the test of Holy Scripture, is one of the most remarkable facts of Church History since the Reformation.

to the so-called seven orders (*Summ. Theol. Suppl.* q. 37.2.c.). The highest order, the fullest order, is that ordained to the celebration of the Eucharist. The bishop does not have any special relation to the Eucharist and does not therefore have any more sacramental authority than a priest. To be sure the episcopate may be called an 'order' in another sense,[1] if order be considered as an office ordained in respect of certain sacred actions such as ordination, but it does not imprint *character* as the priesthood does (*Summ. Theol. Suppl.* q. 35.2.c.; q. 37.2; q. 38.2 ad 2; q. 40.5 ad 2). In other words, still in the language of Roman theology, the episcopal 'order' is not a Sacrament, but only 'sacramental' because it does not derive from Christ but derives only from the Church (*Summ. Theol.* 2.2. q. 184.6 ad 1; 111 q. 67.2 ad 2; q. 82.1 ad 4). In the nature of the case a man cannot be consecrated Bishop unless he has already been ordained priest, and so the difference between the terms 'ordination' and 'consecration' is not haphazard but completely significant. In the full and proper sense *order* has to do with the Sacrament of the Eucharist: that is the essential ministry, and to that nothing by way of ecclesiastical rank can add anything at all.

This doctrine of the *seven* orders, including the episcopate under the order of the presbyterate, was adopted at the Council of Trent, but the superiority of bishops over presbyters in the hierarchy was strongly affirmed (*Denzinger, Enchiridion Symbolorum,* 956aff).

A divergent view was introduced into the Western Church by Duns Scotus who held that the episcopate is not merely sacramental but a Sacrament deriving from a Dominical ordinance, handed down through the Apostles as from Paul to Timothy.[2] There are, therefore, not seven but *eight* orders. Thus against the view of St. Thomas Duns Scotus propounded a view of the episcopate as a real order in the proper sense and therefore a higher order than that of the presbyterate in the ordering of the Eucharist.[3] If so, then the Eucharist

---

[1] *Episcopatus non est ordo, nisi secundum quod ordo officium quoddam est ad sacras actiones. Suppl. q.* 40.5.0. So also Bonaventura: *Episcopatus, prout concernit ordinem sacerdotii, bene potest dici ordo, sed prout distinguitur contra sacerdotium dicit dignitatem quandam vel officium episcopi annexum. Sent* IV.d.24. p. 2, q. 3.

[2] *Si autem conferre non sit simpliciter excellentissimus actus in ecclesia, sed posse constituere aliquem in illa eminentia, cui competit talis actus, tunc non sunt tantum septem ordines sed octo, quia episcopatus tunc est specialis gradus et ordo in ecclesia, cuius est ordines omnes conferre et per consequens omnes in istis eminentibus constituere. Sent* IV.d.24. q. 1.9.

[3] *Sent.* IV.d.24.1.7.

definitely comes under the control of a hierarchy of order, whereas in point of fact, as we have seen, the *eucharistic parousia* cannot be managed, so that even when we bring our various *charismata* to its ordering, in the last resort it is the Lord who orders His own Table, and graciously grants us to serve as deacons or waiters at it. Therefore even in regard to episcopal ordination St. Thomas can say: *Nec dedit ordinem, sed Deus (Summ. Theol.* III. q. 82.8.c. et ad 2).

There lies behind all this a very important Biblical tradition that goes right back to the Mosaic rites of consecration to the Aaronic priesthood (Exod. 28, 29; Lev. 6.9ff; 7.1ff; 8.1ff; Num. 8.1ff). The whole of Israel was regarded as a Kingdom of priests to God (Exod. 19.6), as God's own son, and first-born (Exod. 4.22). But, as we have already had occasion to note, the priesthood of the first-born which was the officiating priesthood in Israel, still apparent in the Passover celebrations, came to be represented and even replaced by an institutional priesthood drawn from the tribe of Levi (Num. 3.12f; 8.19f).

The general term used for their ordination in the Septuagint is ἁγιάζειν, to sanctify, but three very distinctive expressions are used to describe that sanctification or consecration to priesthood (cf. Exod. 29.9f): (*a*) to clothe with priestly garments, to 'put on' (which included the rite of solemn ablution or baptism); (*b*) 'to anoint' with holy oil, given along with the sprinkling of blood; and (*c*) 'to fill the hands' with the special offering for consecration, portions of which were later eaten by the priests as θυσία αἰνέσεως σωτηρίου (Lev. 7.12f). Of these three it was the third which came to be the most distinctive term for ordination, for it was in this part of the rite that the priest's consecration was brought to its fulfilment as he engaged in the sacrificial oblations for the first time.[1] In the Septuagint the Hebrew expression מִלֵּא יַד was translated either by πληροῦν τὰς χεῖρας or by τελειοῦν τὰς χεῖρας (Lev. 7.29; Exod. 28.41; 29.33, etc.). The awkwardness of the former in Greek[1] led to the prevalence of the latter expression which is found in the Epistle to the Hebrews (Heb. 7.28; 9.9; 10.1f) and in the Fourth Gospel (John 17.16f; cf. 17.23).

[1] It is just possible that the πλήρωμα of Eph. 3.19 refers to this. Certainly the same idea is found in the προσαγωγή of Eph. 2.18; 3.12. Is John 3.34, 35 intended to translate מִלֵּא יַד? Certainly the Baptism of Jesus was regarded as His consecration to Messianic Priesthood. Cf. John 6.27. See also John 4.34; 5.36; 17.2f.

Behind these passages lies the fact that in the Old Testament rite of consecration the High Priest alone was anointed as the *christos* (Lev. 4.3f; 6.12f), though the sons of his house were sprinkled with his anointing oil. They were consecrated in and through his self-consecration and were given participation in it, in offering together with him portions of the sacrifice and the bread of consecration, and in sharing with him the meal of consecration. That conception finds a place in our Lord's high-priestly prayer (John 17.1ff).[1] For the sake of the disciples He has sanctified Himself (ὑπὲρ αὐτῶν ἐγὼ ἁγιάζω ἐμαυτόν) that they might be sanctified in truth, and He prays therefore that they may be consecrated together in one (ἵνα ὦσιν τετελειωμένοι εἰς ἕν). Similarly in the Epistle to the Hebrews the high-priestly consecration of Christ in His Self-oblation consecrates all who come to God by Him. Christ has once and for all consecrated us as priests, so that we may draw near to God having our bodies washed with pure water and our hearts sprinkled from an evil conscience (Heb. 10.19f). Christ was the Son of the House of God, the first-born Priest, and in Him the Church of the baptised and consecrated is the Church of the first-born (Heb. 12.23).

Here we have clearly taught a doctrine of the priesthood of the whole Church through its participation in the substitutionary Self-consecration of Christ our High Priest, and Baptism is interpreted in terms of the priestly ablution in the Tabernacle or Temple. Hence the term τελείωσις came later to be used of Baptism. But it was also used of ordination, which would seem to be the natural fulfilment of the Old Testament rite. A step in that direction is already apparent in Heb. 13.15: 'By him let us offer the sacrifice of praise to God continually', which transposes to interpret the Eucharist the rite in which the newly consecrated priests partook of the sacrificial portions of the 'fill-offering' as a 'sacrifice of praise' (Lev. 7.12f). The careful precision of the Epistle is rudely violated when the actual offering of the 'fill-offering' is transferred to the eucharistic offering of bread and wine.

Out of this there arises very properly a theology of ordination in which the climax, so to speak, of the rite of ordination is

---

[1] Evidently Jesus had in mind throughout Lev. 6-8 which was read in preparation for the Passover, along with Jer. 7 which Jesus had in mind in cleansing the Temple. Cf. J. Lightfoot, *Harmony of the Evangelists*, Luke 1.5.

reached, not in the laying on of hands, nor in the devolution of the commission, but in the actual celebration of the Eucharist. It is as *Christ fills the hands* of the presbyter with the bread and wine that his ordination is properly realised and validated. Thus, to use the language of St. Thomas, 'the Sacrament of order is in order to the Eucharist, which is the Sacrament of Sacraments'. In the last analysis it is Christ Himself who is the one Priest, and men are ordained only in the sense that He gives them to share in His Priesthood, but to share in it *alius rationis*, in a mode appropriate to those who are but stewards and servants.

To gather this up so far, we may put it thus: In the Old Testament Church there was a twofold priesthood, the priesthood of the whole body through initiation by circumcision into the royal priesthood, although that priesthood actually functioned through the first-born. Within that royal priesthood there was given to Israel an institutional priesthood in the tribe of Levi, and within that tribe, the house of Aaron. The purpose of the institutional priesthood was to serve the royal priesthood, and the purpose of the royal priesthood, that is of Israel as a kingdom of priests, was to serve God's saving purpose for all nations. So with the Christian Church. The real priesthood is that of the whole Body, but within that Body there takes place a membering of the corporate priesthood, for the edification of the whole Body, to serve the whole Body, in order that the whole Body as Christ's own Body may fulfil His ministry of reconciliation by proclaiming the Gospel among the nations. Within the corporate priesthood of the whole Body, then, there is a particular priesthood set apart to minister to the edification of the Body until the Body reaches the fulness of Christ (Eph. 4.13). Thus in the time of the ascension, in the eschatological reserve between the beginning of the Christian Church at Pentecost and what the Apocalypse calls 'the Marriage-Supper of the Lamb' (Rev. 19.9; cf. 20.1f; 22.17) the Church is served by a ministry in Word and Sacrament. This ministry is as essential to the Church as Bible and sacramental ordinances, but like them, this order of the ministry will pass away at the *parousia*, when the real priesthood of the one Body, as distinct from the institutional priesthood, will be fully revealed.

Orders in the Church thus form a 'scaffolding' in space and

time, as Professor Schmaus has called it (op. cit., p. 572f), for the building up of the Body of Christ as an Habitation of God, but they are also the luminous signs within this world through which, as they are subordinated to the Real Presence of Christ in Word and Sacrament, the true being of the Church as Body of Christ is manifested as far as it may be within empirical history.

So far as a doctrine of order is derived from the Sacrament (in which we see the real priesthood of the Church to derive from Baptismal incorporation, and the particular priesthood in the Church to arise out of the ordering of the eucharistic fellowship), we can agree with the teaching of St. Thomas and join his followers in opposing Scotist error. 'The essential ministry' in the Church, if we are to use that expression, refers to the ministry of Word and Sacrament, and it is such an order of the ministry that it is itself ordered and validated by the Real Presence of Christ in the Eucharist. But we differ from the Roman teaching in regard to the form of the priesthood and the nature of its precise relation to the unique Priesthood of Christ. These differences are of such magnitude that they cannot be passed over lightly.

The form of priesthood in the Church derives from the Form of Christ as the Form of the Suffering Servant. That applies primarily to the whole Church which, as we have seen, is baptised with Christ's own Baptism, baptised into His servant-existence and ministry.

As applied to the whole Church that is remarkably set forth in three successive chapters of the Acts of the Apostles. In the seventh chapter we are given an account of Stephen who before his martyrdom recapitulated in speech the theological history of Israel as the people of the Covenant, but who in his martyrdom recapitulated the essential experience of prophetic Israel as the suffering servant. In a startling way Stephen's martyrdom links up the suffering witness of the Old Testament prophet, with the suffering witness of the servant of Jesus.[1] In the eighth chapter we are given an account of Philip expounding to the Ethiopian the fifty-third chapter of Isaiah, which for the Christian Church is the central chapter on the

[1] Cf. Matt. 5.11f: 'Blessed are ye when men shall revile and persecute you, and shall say all manner of evil against you falsely for my sake. Rejoice and be exceeding glad, for great is your reward in heaven, for so persecuted they the prophets which were before you.'

Suffering Servant. Does this refer to Israel as a whole collectively, or does it refer to the prophet himself? Or does it refer to some other, to the individual Messiah? In some ways it clearly refers to Israel as a whole, in other ways it certainly refers to the Messiah Himself. And yet there is no doubt too that behind the imagery there is the figure of Moses (who in the previous chapter in Acts has been called 'redeemer', its only occurrence in the New Testament), and the prophet's own experience comes into it all which, like that of Jeremiah, is a pointer to what the Messiah Himself in His uniqueness will suffer for the sake of all Israel. In the ninth chapter of the Acts we have a clear and startling answer to those questions. Saul representing official Israel is persecuting the Church, which he was later to call 'the Israel of God' (Gal. 6.16), but on the road to Damascus he encounters the crucified Christ risen again from the dead, who says: 'Saul, Saul, why persecutest thou me?' 'Who art thou, Lord?' 'I am Jesus, whom thou persecutest.' Jesus the crucified identifies Himself with the Church. In the strictest and most concentrated sense Jesus is Israel wholly embodied in His own person, and yet the Church is Israel. Here we have the central mystery of the Incarnation and the Kingdom: Jesus Christ is One and yet Many. And so St. Paul was to write afterwards: 'For as the body is one, and has many members, and all the members of that one body, being many, are one body: so also is Christ' (1 Cor. 12.12). Jesus Christ is Himself the Son of God incarnate in our flesh, and yet He is not alone. He bodies Himself forth in the Church and makes the Church His Body, incorporates it into Himself, so that He can identify Himself with His Church on the ground of His servant-ministry on the Cross.

Three days later St. Paul was baptised, but not according to the rites of Jewish Baptism which was always self-administered except in the instances of infant children and slaves.[1] He was baptised by another into the Name of the Lord Jesus

---

[1] See *Bab. Jebamoth* 46a (Soncino edit. p. 300f). In Judaism baptism of a proselyte meant the complete cancellation of all previous ties and relationships (cf. 2 Cor. 5.17 where Paul uses the language of Judaism in this respect) but that left the Jews a problem in the proselytisation of slaves who would thus always be baptised into freedom in which they were dead to the old ties of slavery. This difficulty was met by enacting that baptism of slaves must be deliberately done into the name of servitude, and by prescribing that whereas normally baptism was self-administered, in the case of a slave he was to be firmly held in the water, and be baptised by his master into his service in Israel.

Christ, after the fashion of a little child or a slave, baptised out of one bondage into another, out of the slavery of sin into the servitude of Christ (Rom. 6.16ff; 1 Cor. 7.21f, etc.). Henceforth Paul called himself a slave of Jesus Christ, separated from his mother's womb (Gal. 1.15), applying to himself the language of the Servant (Isa. 44.2, 24; 49.1, 5; Jer. 1.4; Eccles. 49.7f). In his Apostolic consciousness Paul is aware that he is called of God to give shape and form to the Church as the Body of Christ (Gal. 4.19, etc.) and it is with that in view that he says: 'I am made a minister (of the Gospel), who now rejoice in my sufferings for you, and fill up that which is in arrears of the afflictions of Christ in my flesh for his body's sake, which is the church: whereof I am made a minister, according to the dispensation of God which is given to me for you, to fulfil the word of God, even the mystery . . . which is Christ in you the hope of glory' (Col. 1.23f; cf. also 2 Cor. 1.4f; 4.1f; Isa. 63.9).

As an Apostle Paul is a masterbuilder building up the Church on the foundation of Christ (1 Cor. 3.10), but the Church thus built is to assume the form of a servant (cf. Acts 13.47; 2 Cor. 6.2; 2 Thess. 1.10; Rom. 8.33f). And so he writes to the Philippians: 'Unto you it is given in the behalf of Christ, not only to believe on him, but also to suffer for his sake; having the same conflict which ye saw in me, and now hear to be in me. If therefore there be any consolation in Christ, if any comfort of love, if any fellowship of the Spirit, if any bowels and mercies, fulfil ye my joy, that ye be likeminded, having the same love, being of one accord, of one mind. . . . Let this mind be in you which was also in Christ Jesus, who being in the form of God thought it not robbery to be equal with God: but made himself of no reputation, and took upon him the form of a servant, and was made in the likeness of man: and being found in fashion as a man, he humbled himself, and became obedient unto death, even the death of the cross' (Phil. 2.29-3.8).

The Church that is baptised into the Name of Christ and into His servant-form in this world, has to work that out analogically in itself in life and witness (Heb. 12.1-4; 13.10f; 1 Pet. 2.12ff). Thus though the ministry of the Church does not in any sense extend the ministry of Christ, and though the priesthood in the Church does not prolong His Priesthood, nevertheless the priesthood in the Church derives its form from the form of the Suffering Servant, and so the ministry of the Church goes back to the historical Jesus, not to extend His vicarious functions but to follow Him as disciples of 'the Son of Man who came not to be ministered unto but to minister and to give his life a ransom for many' (Matt. 20.28; Mark 10.45; cf. 1 Tim. 2.4f, which is to be read as a comment on this saying).

In Luke's Gospel and in John's Gospel that teaching is explicitly related by Jesus to the Last Supper. In the latter (John 13.1-17) it is explicitly related to Baptism through which the disciples have part with Christ (cf. Mark 10.38f). That participation is renewed in the feet-washing at the Supper, in token also of their participation in His servant-ministry. 'Ye call me Master, and Lord: and ye say well; for so I am. If I then your Lord and Master, have washed your feet, ye also ought to wash one another's feet. For I have given you an example (ὑπόδειγμα) that ye should do as I have done unto you. Verily, verily, I say unto you, The servant is not greater than his lord; neither he that is sent greater than he that sent him (cf. Matt. 10.25). If ye know these things, happy are ye if ye do them' (John 13.13-17). Here it is made clear that while the form or *hypodeigma* of the Church's ministry derives from that of Christ, it is related to Him nevertheless in terms of the relation of disciple to the Master, of servant to the Lord, of apostle to Christ. In the Lukan account (Luke 22.24ff) the emphasis falls elsewhere. The disciples who have continued with Christ in His temptations are instituted into a royal priesthood in the New Covenant and in the New Israel (Luke 22.28-30), but they are enjoined not to exercise their ministry in history after the fashion of Gentile monarchs, that is, as lords and patrons exercising authority over others, but on the contrary they are to exercise their ministry in humble self-effacement like waiters at a table, that is, like deacons at the Table of the Lord (Luke 22.24-27).

How are we to relate that teaching to the Church's commission from the ascended Lord? We recall that after His triumph over the cross Christ was enthroned at God's right hand, there to continue in grace and omnipotence His ministry as King, Priest, and Prophet, for He is King over all, He ever lives to make high-priestly intercession for us, and from His throne and mercy-seat He sends forth His Spirit through whom

85

He, the incarnate and risen Word, continues to speak and act in the midst of His Church on earth. In entire subordination to the kingly session of Christ on the throne of God and to His heavenly ministry, the Church is sent out into history in the name of Christ, to *serve* Him. This Church is not yet the Church triumphant, judging angels (1 Cor. 6.3) or even the twelve tribes of Israel (Luke 22.30). It does not yet wear the crown that is laid up for it in Christ (2 Tim. 4.8, etc.). It is still the Church militant, and as such the suffering servant on earth, crowned not with a mitre but with thorns like its Master ('It is enough for the disciple that he be as his Master, and the servant as his Lord', Matt. 10.25), for this Church militant is the Church under the Cross, bearing the Cross. If it suffers with Christ it *will reign* with Him (2 Tim. 2.12), and of that the Church already has a glorious anticipation in its sufferings for Christ. Just as the New Testament speaks of Christ's humiliation, His uplifting (ἀνάλημψις, Luke 9.51) on the Cross of shame, as already His exaltation in prelude to His ascension to the throne above (ὑψοῦν—John 3.14; 8.28; 12.32, 34; Acts 2.33; 5.31)[1] so the Church sees in its fellowship with the servant-ministry of Christ and the suffering witness that that involves on earth, its participation already in His exaltation (Matt. 23.12; Luke 14.11; 18.14; 2 Cor. 11.7; Jer. 4.10; 1 Pet. 5.6). Nowhere is that more apparent than in the heart of the Eucharist in the fraction of the bread and in the shedding of the wine through which the Church on earth lifts up its heart (*sursum corda*) on high, for through the Spirit it is made to sit with Christ in heavenly places (Eph. 2.20; 3.6).

That is the heavenly glory that already overflows into the eucharistic fellowship of the Church, but at the Eucharist the Church is given to drink the Cup of Christ and is renewed in His Baptism, proclaiming His death till He come. What the Church does at the Table in communion with the Body of Christ broken for the world and in communion with the Blood of Christ shed in propitiation for the sins of the whole world, the Church is commanded to act out in its life and ministry, and if need be, to be broken in its own body and to shed its own blood for Christ's sake and the Gospel's. Thus although

---

[1] It is from exaltation in this double sense of humiliation and ascension on high that Christ sends down His Spirit ἐξ ὕψους, Luke 24.49; Eph. 4.8. Christ is described in terms of Melchizedek as ἱερεὺς τοῦ θεοῦ ὑψίστου.

the Church is redeemed from the powers of this world and redeemed from the curse of the law, it is sent out from Christ, and from every participation at the Lord's Table, to carry out its mission ὑπὸ νόμον, in the sense that there are conditions and limitations belonging to our creaturely existence under judgment, and also imposed upon us in the kingdoms of this world, which define the limitations under which the Church is to exercise its ministry as the Body of Christ crucified and risen, for these become the very means within history whereby the Church can act out from day to day its implication in the death of Christ and in His servant-ministry. Only as the Church lets itself be implicated in Christ's death and in His reproach, can it minister in His ministry. Only as it learns to let the mind of Christ be in its mind, and is inwardly and outwardly shaped by His servant-obedience unto the death of the Cross, can it participate in His Prophetic, Priestly, and Kingly Ministry. It is in utter self-humiliation in κένωσις, in ταπείνωσις, that the Church can follow in the steps of the Son of Man. It must be prepared to be so conformed to Him whose visage was marred more than any man's (Isa. 52.14; 53.2f). Not by standing on its dignity, or vaunting its rights, not by lordly rule or by patronage, not by any wielding of worldly authority and glory, can the Church effectively fulfil its ministry, but by renouncing all these as the temptations of Satan (Matt. 4.1ff; Luke 4.1ff; Mark 1.12f). It is when the Church is ready to be made of no reputation that it is ready to participate in Christ's own ministry. This is a ministry that is to be exercised only in the weakness of God which is stronger than men (1 Cor. 1.17-31).

The conception of the Suffering Servant is the great characteristic of the Church's ministry, and it is that which above all determines the nature of priesthood in the Church. That applies to the Church's threefold participation in Christ's Prophetic, Priestly, and Kingly Ministry, for the Church is engaged in all these as servant bearing the Cross like the man of Cyrene (Matt. 27.32). It is indeed in terms of the suffering servant-ministry that we are to see the basic unity in the Church's prophetic, priestly, and kingly functions.

V

THE CORPORATE EPISCOPATE

A BIBLICAL doctrine of the episcopate must conform to three cardinal facts or principles.

(a) Jesus Christ alone is the Head of the Church, and presides over it in all things (Col. 1.18; 2.10; Eph. 1.22; 4.15; 5.23).

(b) The ministry is a gift of the ascended Head to the Body, and as such is placed within the Body. It is essentially a sub-ministration which by its very place and nature must not seek to dominate or lord it over the Body, i.e. to usurp the place of the Head. As placed within the Body the ministry is essentially corporate, and must manifest a unity in the Body corresponding to its One Head.

(c) All members of the Body are joined together by the One Spirit in such a way that they are ordered by the Head according to a diversity of function and in a mutual subordination of love.

Those were the principles that Calvin found to be given in the teaching of the New Testament, particularly in the passages, such as Ephesians 4.4-16, where St. Paul speaks of the ministry as the membering of the Body under the disposition of Christ the Head. 'Christ, by His ascension, took away His visible presence from us, and yet He ascended that He might fill all things: now, therefore, He is present in the Church, and always will be. When Paul would show the mode in which He exhibits Himself, he calls our attention to the ministerial offices which He employs: "Unto every one of us is given grace according to the measure of the gift of Christ"; "And He gave some, apostles, and some prophets, and some evangelists, and some pastors and teachers" (Eph. 4.10, 7, 11).' (*Instit.* 4.6.10; 4.1.5; 4.3.1; 4.3.1ff.)

The Church is Christ's Kingdom which He rules by the sceptre of His Word (*Instit.* 4.2.4) and over which He presides as the One Bishop (*Instit.* 4.2.6; 4.6.17; cf. 4.6.4).[1] As such He

---

[1] In all three passages Calvin cites the *De simplicitate praelatorum* attributed to Cyprian, for its doctrine of the one Episcopate of Christ.

bestows upon the Church the gift of the ministry. It is the frail earthen vessel in which He has deposited the keys of the Kingdom, or the heavenly treasure of the Gospel (*Instit.* 4.1.1, 5, 20, 22; 4.3.1, etc.). Calvin has such an exalted understanding of the ministry that he says 'God Himself appears, and as the author of this ordinance requires His presence to be recognised in His own institution' (*Instit.* 4.1.5). It is the mode in which the ascended Lord comes to His Church and exhibits Himself in it (*Instit.* 4.6.10). Christ can be described, therefore, as 'using the ministry of men *quasi vicariam operam*', and 'of employing men to perform the function of His ambassadors, to be interpreters of His secret will who, in short, *personam suam repraesentent* (*Instit.* 4.3.1). 'In this way Christ exhibits Himself as in a manner actually present by exerting the energy of His Spirit in this His institution' (*Instit.* 4.3.2).

Among others Calvin sees three purposes in Christ's choice of this mode of presence in His Church. It means that He comes to us *humanitus*, 'for He consults our weakness, being pleased to address us after the manner of men (*humano more*), instead of driving us away by His thunder' (*Instit.* 4.1.5). Again, by binding us to the ministry of one another He has forged 'a sacred bond of unity' (*Instit.* 4.1.5). 'The Lord has astricted His Church to what He foresaw would be the strongest bond of unity when He deposited the doctrine of eternal life and salvation with men, that by their hands He might communicate it to others (Eph. 4.4f)' (*Instit.* 4.3.1). Further, 'it forms a most excellent and useful training to humility, when He accustoms us to obey His Word though preached by men like ourselves, or, it may be, our inferiors in worth' (*Instit.* 4.3.1).

This ministry in the Church is described as 'a subministration diffused throughout all the members, while the power flows from one celestial Head' (*Instit.* 4.6.9). 'See how all men without exception are placed in the body, while the honour and name of Head are left to Christ alone' (Eph. 4.15f). 'See how to each member is assigned a certain measure, a finite and limited function, while both the perfection of grace and the supreme power of government reside only in Christ.' 'He attributes nothing to men but a common ministry, and a special mode to each' (*ibid.*).

Calvin speaks of Ephesians 4 as giving a 'complete representation of that sacred and celestial government to which posterity has given the name of hierarchy' (*ibid.*). But he also points us to the 'form of the early Church', 'which sets before our eyes, as it were, *an image of the divine institution*' (*divinae institutionis imaginem*). 'For although the bishops of those times published many canons, in which they seemed to express more than is expressed in the sacred volume, yet they were so cautious in framing all their economy on the Word of God, the only standard, that it is easy to see that in scarcely any respect they departed from it' (*Instit.* 4.4.1).

When we ask what this order was, Calvin refers to 'the order of *presbyters* to whom the office of teaching was committed'. 'In each city these presbyters selected one of their number to whom they gave the special title *bishop*, lest, as usually happens, from equality dissension should arise. The bishop, however, was not so superior in honour and dignity as to have dominion over his colleagues, but as it belongs to a president in an assembly to bring matters before them, collect their opinions, take precedence of others in consulting, advising, exhorting, guide the whole procedure by his authority, and execute what is decreed by common consent, a bishop held the same office in a meeting of presbyters' (*Instit.* 4.4.2). This order, Calvin points out, citing Jerome, was introduced 'more by custom than in consequence of our Lord's appointment' (*ibid.*, Jerome, *ad Tit.* 1). Thus 'each presbyter, merely to preserve order and peace, was under one bishop, who, though he excelled others in dignity, was subject to the meeting of the brethren' (*Instit.* 4.4.2). 'In the public meeting, the bishops had some dress to distinguish them from the other presbyters. Presbyters, also, and deacons, were ordained by the laying on of hands; but each bishop, with the college of presbyters, ordained his own presbyters. But although they all did the same act, yet because the bishop presided, and the ordination was performed as it were under his auspices, it was said to be his. Here ancient writers often say that a presbyter does not differ in any respect from a bishop except in not having the power of ordaining' (*Instit.* 4.4.15).[1]

The distinctive feature about this doctrine of the episcopate

[1] Essentially the same teaching is to be found in the works of Martin Bucer. See especially the following: *Von der waren Seelsorge, Ein summarischer Vergriff, De vi et usu sacri ministerii, De Regno Christi* 1.5; 2.8, and *De ordinatione legitima*. The last two were written specifically for the Church of England and their influence is still apparent in the Anglican *Ordinal*.

is that Calvin seeks to hold together in it equality of ministers before God and yet distinction in place and authority within the presbytery. 'The political distinction of ranks is not to be repudiated, for natural reason itself dictates this in order to take away confusion; but that which shall have this object in view, will be so arranged that it may neither obscure Christ's glory nor minister to ambition or tyranny, nor prevent all ministers from cultivating mutual fraternity with each other, with equal rights and liberties' (*Comm. on Num.* 3.5). Calvin does allow a certain power of authority to bishops, but it resides 'partly in bishops and partly in councils' (*Instit.* 4.8.1). 'I speak only of spiritual power', he adds, 'which is proper to the Church, and which consists in doctrine, or jurisdiction, or in enacting laws. . . . Whatever is taught respecting the power of the Church ought to have reference to the end for which Paul declares (2 Cor. 10.8; 13.10) that it was given, namely, for edification and not for destruction, those who use it lawfully deeming themselves to be nothing more than servants of Christ, and, at the same time, servants of the people in Christ. Moreover, the only mode by which ministers can edify the Church is, by studying to maintain the authority of Christ, which cannot be unimpaired, unless that which He received of the Father is left to Him, viz., to be the only Master of the Church' (*Instit.* 4.8.1).

Two factors have to be taken into account here, and in regard to both of them, Calvin is indebted to Cyprian. The first is that the ministry in the Church is involved in the mode of connexion by which believers are united with Christ the Head (*Instit.* 4.6.10). The inseparable connexion which all members of Christ have with each other in His Body lies behind the whole conception of the episcopate as a subministration of 'the One Bishopric of Christ' (*Instit.* 4.2.6 citing *De simplic. Praelat.*). 'All the health or life which is diffused throughout the members flows from the Head, so that the members occupy a subordinate rank. By the distribution made, the limited share of each renders the communication between all the members absolutely necessary. Without mutual love, the health of the Body cannot be maintained' (*Comm. on Eph.* 4.16). Arising out of this comes the fact that the episcopate in the Church is held *in solidum* by the ministers. 'Cyprian claims the Bishopric for Christ alone leaving the administration of it to individuals but in a united capacity, no one being permitted to exalt himself above others' (*Comm. on Eph.* 4.11, citing Cyprian's *De unitate ecclesiae* 2; see also the *Antidote to Articles of the Faculty of Sacred Theol. of Paris,* 23; *Instit.* 4.6.17, etc.). That is the doctrine of *the corporate episcopate.*

This does not mean that Calvin held that the priesthood of the Church is dissolved in the general body of believers. Rather is the priesthood of the Church imaged in the midst of the community of believers in the form of a divinely instituted ministry, an episcopate held in a united capacity by those called and ordained to the ministry of Word and Sacraments. This episcopate is placed within the Body and partakes of its inner cohesion in mutual service and love, but at the same time it involves diversities of function and distinctions in order, through which Christ exhibits Himself as actually present in the Church as its only Bishop and Master. The ordering of the ministry cannot be separated from the real presence of Christ in the Lordship of the Word, nor can it be separated from the Body within which it is placed and has its mode of function.

What is called in question here is the notion of *hierarchy,* not perhaps as it was held in the ancient Catholic Church (*Instit.* 4.4.3; 4.6.10), but as it came to be interpreted in the subtle speculations of the Pseudo-Dionysius (*Instit.* 1.14.4), and by Rome (*Instit.* 4.4.4; 4.6.17), where the hierarchical ordering of the Church and its ministry on earth is regarded as a transcription of a heavenly pattern. When that idea is clamped down upon the ministry of the Church it alienates it entirely from the teaching of the New Testament and from the teaching of the ancient Catholic Church. Calvin holds that the episcopate, as a subministration diffused throughout the whole Body and held *in solidum* by the ministry of bishops and presbyters, is an image of the divine institution, but a hierarchic ordering of that imports into it a notion of monarchy which conflicts with the mode of connexion which members of the Body have with one another. It gives the episcopate a mediatorial function independent of the Church as the Body of Christ. Such a notion of hierarchy strikes at the root of the corporate priesthood of the whole Church as the Body of Christ. It isolates the episcopate from the Body and makes the Body hang upon a self-perpetuating and self-sufficient institution. On the other hand the notion of hierarchy posits such a reciprocal relation between the celestial hierarchy and the ministry of the Church on earth that it allows the episcopate to presume control over the Kingdom of Christ.

It is illuminating to see that *hierarchy* was not an isolated notion in the development of the orders of the Church. It belonged to a whole movement in which a Neo-Platonic doctrine of μίμησις and εἶδος came to be applied to Christian life and thought.

That is very apparent in the realm of art, for example. The earliest Christian Art in the catacombs was essentially *signitive* and *sacramental* (cf. Wladimir Weidlé, *The Baptism of Art*, p. 8ff). That is to say, it was content with a curt realistic painting used in a sacramental context to pass on a meaning not embodied in the artistic forms. Thus a painting of the Good Shepherd could borrow the figure of Hermes Criophoros taken from contemporary art, but very little attempt was made, apart from the clear Biblical setting, to reshape the outward figure to conform to the reality intended in Christ. Here the relation between the sign and thing signified belonged to a divine mystery, in which the sign was used to point quite beyond itself. The power of this art did not lie in any fusion of form and content but in the *anamnesis* of the Gospel. It was thus essentially a sacramental mode of signification in which the earthly sign in some measure corresponds to the heavenly reality, but in comparison with which the signs are nothing in themselves, for they carry us altogether beyond themselves and convey what can never be reduced to our earthly forms.

That art soon began to disappear after the Constantinian establishment and gave way to art of a different sort in which form and content were fused. That is particularly apparent in the *ikons* of the Eastern Church. At first the *ikon* was but an image (εἴκων) of an Apostle or saint, but that came to be set in a context where it was contemplated *sub specie aeternitatis*, and then under the influence of Platonic notions of εἶδος and μίμησις, the *ikon* was regarded as having in some way hypostatic relation to the Apostle or saint himself: it was a hypostatic transcription or μίμησις of the heavenly reality, claiming veneration on earth.

The theology behind that derives, apparently, from the Platonising tendencies long at work in Alexandria. If a purely

Platonic relation between eternity and time is envisaged, in which the temporal is but a transient image of the eternal, then the notion of the everlasting Gospel lifts the gravity of significance away altogether from the historical Gospel. In that event there arises a docetic interpretation of the historical Jesus and the historical sacrifice on the Cross, and exegesis is bound to give a 'demythologised' interpretation of the Gospel. There are two ways out of that impasse: either to go back to the Biblical understanding of the relation between the eternal and the temporal, or to carry on beyond the merely Platonic conception and posit a reciprocal relation between the eternal and the temporal, the heavenly and the earthly, at least in the Church. That was the line usually taken, which helped the Church to recover something of the historical Christ out of the rationalistic demythologisation demanded by the *Logos* Christologies, but which imparted to the doctrine of the Sacraments, and so to the doctrine of the ministry, a radical change. Here we have (*a*) a fusion of form and content, and along with it, (*b*) a reciprocal relation between the earthly and the heavenly. That reached its great climax in the Tridentine doctrine of transubstantiation in the Mass and the corresponding conception of the hierarchical priesthood of the Church. In reaction to that whole development, the Reformation of the Church in the sixteenth century sought to restore the true face of the Church by reaching back to the teaching of the New Testament and of the old Catholic Fathers.

At this point we may gather up some of the ideas in our discussion so far as they are relevant to the doctrine of the corporate episcopate. The Church as the Body of Christ *participates* in Christ's Prophetic, Priestly, and Kingly ministry by *serving* Him. The Church's ministry may be described as a corporate priesthood of the Many reposing substitutionarily in the One Priest, the One Mediator between God and man, the Man Christ Jesus. The pattern of this relation between the priesthood of the Church and the Priesthood of Christ is to be described in terms of *hypodeigma*: a pattern put forward in the Church for observation, signifying a higher reality. By employing this term the Fourth Gospel directs the Church to the example of Christ in the Form of a Servant, while the Epistle to the Hebrews, in its employment of this term instead of the terms *paradeigma* and *eidos*, expressly rejects a Platonic interpretation of the relation between the heavenly Priesthood of Christ and the priesthood of the Church in terms of *mimesis*.

Two further illustrations from the New Testament will help us here.

(*a*) In Romans 8 where Paul speaks of the heavenly intercession of Christ at the right hand of God (8.34f), where He holds us in a bond of divine love from which nothing can separate us, he also speaks of the bearing of that upon the worship of the Church through the Spirit who helps our infirmities (8.26f). 'We know not what to pray for as we ought, but the Spirit himself makes intercessioñs for us with groanings that cannot be uttered. He that searches the hearts knows what is the mind of the Spirit, because he makes intercession for the saints according to the will of God.' In other words, through the Spirit the heavenly intercession of Christ is echoed unutterably in the stammering intercessions of the Church on earth— *unutterably*. Our prayers are in no sense transcriptions in the language of earth of the heavenly liturgy around the throne of God, nevertheless they are related to that inexpressible mystery in the Spirit.

(*b*) The Apocalypse supplies us with a close parallel, not only in regard to 'the prayers of the saints' (Rev. 8.3f), but in regard to the whole liturgy of heaven and earth.[1] In Patmos, in the Spirit on the Lord's Day, John is apparently thinking of the liturgy of the Eucharist, perhaps at Ephesus, for fragmented snatches of that break through the account of his apocalyptic visions. He looks through an open door in heaven and is given to see and hear the liturgy around the enthroned Lamb described as the Song of Moses and of the Lamb. As in the Epistles to the Romans and to the Hebrews, so in the Apocalypse, there is the closest relation between the eucharistic worship of the Church on earth and the eternal intercession of Christ at the right hand of God where all the hosts of heaven as liturgical spirits join in praise and thanksgiving. But of that heavenly music the liturgy on earth is only an *echo*. The liturgy of heaven centres in the Self-presentation of the Lamb of God before the Father. He is our Saviour through whose sacrifice and blood we are redeemed. The Church in its eucharistic liturgy does not participate in that sacrifice except by echoing it in the

[1] For a fuller exposition see *Liturgy and Apocalypse, Church Service Society Annual*, 1954.

counter-sacrifice of praise and thanksgiving. He, the Lamb, is *upon* the altar-throne, and He only is able to open the book of destiny and undo guilt and sin, but the saints are given to pray *beneath* the altar. In other words, the eucharistic sacrifice in the liturgy of the Church on earth belongs to a different dimension; it is an echo of the sacrifice of Christ made on our behalf. It is the joyful communion of those who give thanks for a sacrifice made on their behalf and who are summoned by the music of angels to an antiphonal oblation of praise and thanksgiving.

As such the liturgy of the Church on earth is essentially imperfect and fragmentary. All we get here are broken snatches of the earthly liturgy as it echoes the heavenly. The heavenly liturgy is described as *the New Song*, which no one knows but the redeemed who have passed over to the other side. On this side, in the fallen world, in the Church militant, it is impossible to score that New Song. The perfect liturgical forms of heaven are in no sense transcribed in the forms of earth, although the ineffable New Song of Heaven keeps breaking in and opening up the ordered liturgical forms of earth to make them point above and beyond themselves. Thus the liturgical forms of earth, no matter how 'perfect and beautiful and adequate we may make them, are ever being judged as earthly by the New Song of Heaven, ever being rendered fragmentary and revealed as essentially imperfect.

That is why there is a *sursum corda* in the heart of the Eucharist. Like St. John in the Spirit on the Lord's Day, we lift up our hearts above and beyond the liturgy of earth and in breathtaking wonder and in indescribable joy echo the heavenly Song of the Lamb. As this fragmentary and imperfect echo of the perfect liturgy and music of heaven the sacramental liturgy of the Church is at once an anticipation of the future, and yet an interim measure that will pass away. It has its place here and now as echo and antepast, but will disappear when the full glory of the heavenly worship will be revealed. Meantime Christian liturgy holds the new wine in old wine-skins, and therefore in all Christian liturgy there is a breaking of the old wine-skins, a judgment upon the very liturgical forms that we use to hold the new wine of the Kingdom.

It is essentially in the same sense and along the same line that we are to understand the relation between the priesthood of the Church on earth and the Priesthood of Christ at the right hand of God, between the episcopate placed within the Body in history, and the Episcopate of the ascended Head of the Church. Through the Spirit there is a direct relation of participation, but in form and order the relation is indirect. The priesthood of the Church is not a transcription in the conditions of this passing age of the heavenly Priesthood of Christ. No transubstantiation or fusion between the two is involved. The relation is truly sacramental and eschatological. The ordered pattern of the ministry is used by Christ as a mode of His Presence in the Church, and so it points beyond itself to His Real Presence. In so doing the pattern of the ministry on earth subjects itself to the impending judgment in the advent of Christ, and acknowledges that it will pass away in order that the perfect pattern of His Kingdom will be revealed. Thus though we may speak of an ordering of the priesthood of the Church in history in terms of a corporate episcopate, that ordering is not a translation into terms of space and time of a heavenly order. If we are to use the term hierarchy that must not be understood as if it were within history a replica of an eternal and celestial reality.

A distinction must be clearly drawn between the corporate priesthood of the Church given to it through baptismal incorporation into Christ, and the special institutional priesthood arising out of the ordering of the eucharistic fellowship and determined by it. This is a special gift of the ascended Lord to the Church for its mission 'in the last times', between Pentecost and the *parousia*.[1] The corporate priesthood of the whole Church endures on into the new creation, transformed in the likeness and glory of Christ, but the corporate episcopate will pass away. It is essentially an expression of the functioning of the corporate priesthood of the Church, given directly by Christ as a gift for the building up of the Church to be an Habitation of God. In the growth of the Body there is erected around the Body, or in the building of the Temple as an Habitation of God, there is erected around it, a temporary scaffolding in the holy ministry. But in the fulness of the Church the whole order of the ministry including all the various *charismata*, as well as

---

[1] Cf. the illuminating discussion of the relation between the ἐπισκοπή of the Church and the eschatological ἐπισκοπή of Christ in His *parousia*, *The Historic Episcopate* (edit. by K. Carey), p. 18.

the Bible and the Sacraments, will pass away. Then the essential form of the Church and the perfect pattern of its worship will be revealed in Christ.

Our problem, however, is within time and within the succession of history between the two advents of Christ in which the Church's prophetic, priestly, and kingly ministry is exercised. How are we to think of the ordering of that ministry? And how are we to think of the orderly relation between the special priesthood in the Church and the priesthood of the whole Body? We must answer those questions in terms of ἐπισκοπή, the special gift of the Spirit for the ordering of the Body and its edification.

We have already examined the two notions of the episcopate in the Western Church, advocated, for example, by Thomas Aquinas and by Duns Scotus. According to St. Thomas the bishop does not belong to another order than that of the presbyter, for he has no more sacramental authority with regard to the Eucharist, the Sacrament of Sacraments, than the presbyter. The bishop is given place over the presbyter, an essential place in the Church, but he does not represent a higher order in the ordering of the Eucharist, or as we would say, in regard to Word and Sacrament. According to the Scotist teaching—and error—the bishop does represent a higher order than the presbyter with respect to the Eucharist. If so, then there is introduced into the ordering of the Eucharist, *just where the liturgy of the Church on earth echoes the liturgy of the heavenly worship*, an essential *hierarchy*, which, logically, must be a replica of a heavenly hierarchy.[1] It is this notion of hierarchy given a theological and Platonic interpretation that lies at the root of so much mischief in the history of the Church. When that in turn is given political interpretation in the State then we have the late Mediaeval doctrine of the episcopate which occasioned the shattering of ecclesiastical unity in the Western Church.

The time has surely come for a reinterpretation of the episcopate in the light of the Church as the Body of Christ, and in terms of the ordering of the eucharistic fellowship. This seems to demand a doctrine of the *corporate episcopate* set in a threefold dimension of depth.

[1] This idea was originally imported into the West through the translation by John Scotus Erigena of the *Celestial Hierarchy* and the *Ecclesiastical Hierarchy* of pseudo-Dionysius.

(a) The foundation of all is baptismal incorporation into Christ involving the royal priesthood of the whole Body. This is priesthood in a secondary sense, not another priesthood than that of Christ (who alone is Priest in the proper sense), but a humble participation of the Church in His Priesthood in terms of service.

(b) Within that royal priesthood there is a special modification of it for the service of the Church, arising out of the ordering of the Lord's Supper. This is instituted and given by Christ to the Church for the ministry of the Word and Sacrament in history. It is the priesthood of order. Because this is within the corporate priesthood of the whole Body, and serves it, this special priesthood must be given a corporate or collegiate expression.

(c) Within and over the priesthood in the Church there is the episcopate, not as a higher priesthood but as a special gift for the oversight of the priesthood, and as the sign both of the corporate nature of the priesthood and of the corporate continuity of the Church.

By Baptism into Christ the Church is adopted to be His Body for He has joined it to Himself in One Spirit, and is pleased to use it as His Body in the world. In a real sense, as we have seen, the Church is yet to become One Body with Christ, in the resurrection, but it has already been sealed in Baptism and hallowed for that purpose. Until that day comes the Church is given the ordinance of the Lord's Supper whereby it continually feeds upon the Body and Blood of Christ and is renewed in its incorporation into Him as His Body. As such it is continually sent out in its bodily existence to fulfil its ministry within the physical world and the succession of time. Thus the concrete forms of the cosmos in space and time are to be used by the Church—the $\sigma\chi\dot{\eta}\mu\alpha\tau\alpha$ $\tau o\hat{v}$ $\kappa o\sigma\mu o\hat{v}$. But while the Church continues to have bodily existence and continuity in this world, it must make use of $\sigma\chi\dot{\eta}\mu\alpha\tau\alpha$ without being schematised to them. 'Be ye not conformed (or schematised) to this world but be ye transformed' (Rom. 12.2). The ordering of the Church cannot therefore be schematised to worldly democracy, aristocracy, monarchy, or anarchy. It has a unique ordering and its relations to the forms of this world is essentially dialectical, because it is sacramental. In other words, because the Church is called to die and rise with Christ, to bear about in its Body the dying

99

of the Lord Jesus that the life also of the Lord Jesus may be made manifest in its Body, that governs its relation to the forms of this world. The Church must learn therefore to die and rise with Christ as often as it partakes of the Eucharist, and renews its Baptism whereby it puts off the old man and puts on the new man. Thus its relation to the forms of this world is in terms of having and not having, using and not misusing, as bound by them and yet free from them.

Within these forms the Church is to be schematised to the law of the Spirit who sheds abroad in the Church the love of God. That love, as we have seen, is ontological fact and refers to the concrete reality of the Church's participation in the New Humanity in Christ. The ordering of this Church given a new being in love must be an ordering correlative to the law of love in the Holy Spirit. That is what St. Paul expounds in 1 Corinthians 12-14, in the relation of the diverse *charismata*. The form which this ordering of the Body takes is the membering of the Body under the disposition of the Head of the Body. Christ is Himself the One and the Many. As the One Head who sends His One Spirit of love He orders the many into membership of the One Body through the Spirit: a membership that coheres in love and operates by love. Thus there is an inner membering of the Church as the Body of Christ, but that inner membering is such that each member is made a member of every other member in a relation of mutuality. Each serves the other and ministers to the edification of the other in the One Body, as the other ministers to his edification in the same Body. It belongs to the essential bodily nature of the Church that each is ministered to by another. That membering rises out of the ordering of the eucharistic fellowship and it has its supreme expression at the Lord's Table where each receives the bread and wine at the hands of another in the Name of Christ in a communion where one without the other is not perfected in love. Spiritually and theologically every one is a deacon at the Lord's Table.

This relation of mutuality arising out of the eucharistic fellowship means not only that we minister to one another, but that we are under authority to one another (cf. 1 Cor. 12.10; 14.29). As the wife has no authority over her own body but the husband, and the husband has no authority over his own body but the wife (1 Cor. 7.4), so in the bodily existence of the Church every member is under authority to every other member and therefore he must not think of himself more highly than he ought. He must think soberly. No one lives for himself or exercises a gift for himself, but for others and unto Christ.

The form which this mutual membering takes is in the diversity and unity of the *charismata*, the special gifts of the Spirit bestowed for the mutual edification of all the members of the Body and for the functioning of the whole Body. Each gift is dependent on the gift of another, and each functions properly only in dependence on a diverse gift. This diversity in mutual dependence knits the membership together. It preserves and enriches the unity of the Church in the manifold grace of God. In the ordering of the diverse gifts, and the functions they involve, a number of principles are indicated.

(1) The primary gift belonging to the foundation of the Church and without which there can be no relation of the Head over the Body is the Apostolic Office. Under this gift all the others are ordered.

(2) All gifts are subordinated to the Word of God, and all assist the ministering of the Word. That arises right out of the Sacraments, for they are the Sacraments of the Word made flesh. In the sacramental enfleshment the Word comes to its full eventuation in our humanity. But in the Church that results from this enfleshment it is the Word which exercises supreme authority, or rather it is Christ in the Sacraments of the Word made flesh, who in His real Presence commands us through His Word and gives in the Sacraments what He commands. Just as the head without the body is useless, so the Word without the Sacraments is an abstraction, and the Sacraments without the Word are a torso. In the unity of Word and Sacrament authority comes from the commanding Word of the Lord. All ministry is given its place accordingly, as a deaconing of that Word made flesh.

(3) All gifts repose upon the gift of love. Diverse gifts are related to it as transient helps and manifestations of the one enduring gift of love. They are designed by the Spirit to the end that they may minister to the edification of the Body in love. All others pass away, along with faith and hope, but love endures on beyond this passing age into the abiding time of the New Creation.

(4) Under the supreme mediation of the Word through the Apostles and within the Body as a community of love, the gifts of the ministry fall into two complementary sorts which come to their most precise distinction in the functions of *deacon* and *presbyter*. As we have seen, all members of the Body are deacons to one another in love in the eucharistic fellowship, but within that there is a distinction of function between that of deacon and that of presbyter. The diaconal ministry and the presbyteral ministry correspond to one another in an essential complementarity like that of wife and husband in the one body. Thus it should not be possible to pass from the diaconal office to the presbyteral or from the presbyteral office to the diaconal, any more than it is possible to pass from the wifely ministry to the husbandly, or from the husbandly ministry to the wifely. The *charisma* of the presbyter is to minister the Word and Sacraments and to shepherd the flock. The *charisma* of the deacon is to prompt and shape the response of the congregation in life and worship, and so to assist the ministry in the application of the Word and in the dispensation of the mysteries. Thus through the deacon the ministry of the presbyter is integrated with the priesthood of the whole Body, and in that integration the presbyter leads the congregation in their *leitourgia* and *latreia* of body and spirit before the face of the Father.

(5) Within the Church some have a *charisma* for oversight or ἐπισκοπή within and over the special qualification of the Church's priesthood in the presbyterate, as well as the diaconate and the whole Church. This is the function of the presbyter-bishop in a ministry that proclaims the eschatological ordering of the whole Church in Christ, until the Chief Shepherd will be manifested in His ἐπισκοπή or visitation. Christ is Himself the *Episcopos* or Bishop of our souls in the supreme sense, but participation in that ministry of Christ is given to the whole presbyterate and exercised in their name by the presiding bishop (προέστως) as the sign of the unity and the continuity of the Church.

To recapitulate: The corporate priesthood in the response of the whole Body to Word and Sacrament is expressed in the ministry of the deacon. Within that corporate priesthood there is the special qualification of it arising out of the Eucharist, where the function of the presbyter is to act *as the shepherd* who feeds the flock through the Word and Sacraments with the

Body and Blood of Christ, *as the leitourgos* who leads the congregation in its rational worship, and *as the watchman* who looks after the spiritual welfare of all and directs them into the unity of the Faith. The bishop does not therefore represent a higher or more special priesthood, but represents the presidency of the whole Body which gathers the special priesthood or presbyterate into a collegiate expression within the corporate priesthood of the whole Body.

In the light of this it would appear proper to work for a mutual adaptation of our churches and a re-ordering of their ministries in such a way as to assimilate into unity the three main aspects of the ministry that appear in churches of the Congregational, Presbyterian, and Episcopal types. In such an adaptation there would take place an integration of the episcopate with the presbytery and an integration of episcopal presbytery with the corporate priesthood of the whole Body.

We may outline that in the following way:

(1) The corporate priesthood of the whole Body involves a membering in the ministry in which every member has a special function to perform, according to the measure of grace given to him, in the life and growth and the Body and its mission in the Evangel. The ordering of this corporate priesthood takes its pattern from the eucharistic fellowship in which each member is a member of the other and every member participates in the deaconing of love. This is given a representative expression in the office of the *deacons* who should therefore have an essential place in the councils of the Church. In the presbytery, for example, deacons representing every parish should have their place along with presbyters sharing with them conjointly the authority of the presbytery.

(2) Within the priesthood that pertains to the whole membership of the Body there is the special qualification of priesthood, the presbyterate, in which some are set apart and are ordained specifically for the ministry of Word and Sacrament and pastoral oversight of the flock of Christ. It is their function to bring the Word of God to the people, to build them up in the Body of Christ, dispensing to them the mysteries of God and leading them in the way of all godliness. This presbyteral ministry within the Body should be articulated in a corporate way: the corporate episcopate in which compresbyters hold the episcopate *in solidum*. This presbyter might be described as

presbyter *in corpore*, who along with his fellow-presbyters exercises conjointly a corporate episcopate within the presbytery, but who within his own parish exercises the full ministry of Word and Sacrament and oversight over the flock committed to his charge.

(3) Also within the presbytery but presiding over it is the bishop who is a fellow-presbyter in the presbytery but who permanently presides over it as bishop. He might be described as bishop *in presbyterio*. In him as president the corporate episcopate is gathered up to a head. As its chief expression he is the sign of the unity and continuity of the whole presbyterate and the whole Church. As such he fulfils a paternal office to the whole flock, to the presbyters and to the congregations under their charge.

It may be a help toward clarification of this suggestion if the difference between the *presbyter in the Church of Scotland* and *presbyter in the Church of England* is noted. In the Church of England the presbyter is regarded as a delegate of the bishop in that he does not hold the episcopate *in solidum* with the bishop. Consequently in the Church of England the episcopate is given an individualist expression in a single bishop. There are, however, relics of an ancient practice in the association of presbyters with the bishop at ordinations, and in the tradition that the pastoral charge of the congregation is shared by the bishop and the presbyter. In the Church of Scotland the presbyter is a presbyter-bishop who along with his fellow-presbyters holds and exercises the episcopate *in solidum* in the *presbytery*. Consequently in the Church of Scotland the episcopate is given a corporate or collegiate expression in the presbytery, known therefore as 'The Rev. the Presbytery'.

It would seem right and proper, and wholly in accord with the Biblical doctrine of the ministry, that this *Presbytery* or *Corporate Episcopate* should be assimilated to what is known as the *Historic Episcopate*. In the integration of the bishop with presbytery both the episcopal and presbyterial traditions would not only be preserved but deepened and enhanced through fuller integration with the royal priesthood of the whole Body and fuller participation in the One Bishopric of Christ.

On this basis the unity and continuity of the Church would be threefold.

(*a*) The unity and continuity of the whole Body baptismally incorporated into the Royal Priesthood of Christ.

(*b*) The unity and continuity therein of the presbytery or the corporate episcopate, including bishop, presbyters, and deacons.

(*c*) The unity and continuity of consecrated bishops, presiding within and over the presbytery, a sign of the unity of the episcopate and the continuity of order.

Two fundamental questions have to be faced here to which due attention must be given by Episcopalians and Presbyterians.

(1) *The place of intercommunion in the mutual adaptation of our churches.* If order is in order to the Sacrament of the Eucharist, the Sacrament of Sacraments, as St. Thomas put it, and is itself ordered by that Sacrament, or, as I would prefer to put it, if the doctrine of order arises out of the ordering of the eucharistic fellowship and is there subordinated to the Real Presence of Christ the Lord of the Church, then we must give far more serious consideration to the place the Lord's Supper occupies in the healing of our disorder. Cogent reasons for that can be offered.

(*a*) No Ecumenical Council of the Church has ever made agreement with regard to the Lord's Supper a prerequisite for unity or for reunion. The Nicene Creed is normative here, which does not mention the Lord's Supper, but which acknowledges 'one Baptism for the remission of sins'.

(*b*) The Sacrament of the Lord's Supper clearly presupposes a prior unity, but that unity is given in Holy Baptism through which we are incorporated into the One Body of Christ. To repudiate intercommunion and thus to perpetuate disunion would surely be to act a lie against Holy Baptism. For a church to refuse the Lord's Supper to those who are baptised into Christ and incorporated into His One Body would seem to amount either to a denial of Baptism or to attempted schism within the Body of Christ.

(*c*) Behind the whole issue of intercommunion lies the fundamental doctrine of Atonement through the Blood of Christ. For churches to refuse to come together at the Lord's Table is surely to deny the sacrifice of Christ, for He loved the Church and died for it to make it one in Him. It is difficult to see how we can go on proclaiming the atonement without being at one among ourselves, or how we can go on proclaiming reconciliation without acting a lie against it if we refuse to be reconciled in the Communion of the Body and Blood of Christ. To hold ourselves back from intercommunion is in point of fact to limit the range and efficacy of the death of Christ.

(*d*) The Sacrament of the Lord's Supper is not merely a cognitive Sacrament acknowledging a prior unity, but it is an effective Sacrament enacting a real unity. Nor is it a Sacrament of our penitence as if the measure of our repentance or lack of repentance in disunion could limit its range and effectiveness. It is the Sacrament of the Body and Blood of Christ in which He gives us repentance and remission of sins. Too many arguments against intercommunion deny the effectuating action of the Lord's Supper and call in question its efficacy to overcome our divisions. If the Sacrament is effective as well as cognitive, then it does not only acknowledge a prior unity but re-enacts it and completes it. How can churches expect to be healed of their divisions if they refuse to take together the very means given by Christ to heal them of their divided and broken estate? Can we expect to take any real step toward unity if we are not prepared to use the Holy Sacrament to apply the healing Cross to the wounds and sins of our divisions? It was to the church at Corinth which had 'schism' at the Eucharist that St. Paul said: 'For this cause there are many weak and sickly among you and many sleep' (1 Cor. 11.30).

(*e*) Much of our division with regard to the Lord's Supper arises from the fact that the Sacrament which reposes in the Person of Christ has been transferred and made to repose upon the Church and its continuity. It has thus become an ecclesiastical Sacrament. No doubt the celebration of the Eucharist is embedded in the institutional continuity of the Church, but by its very nature as the Sacrament of the Real Presence of Christ it stands above the institutional continuity of the Church, and can never be made relative to it, for that would make the Church the master of Christ's presence and not Christ the Master of the Church.[1] The Sacrament is the Lord's Supper and not a private rite of this or that church, so that at the Sacrament all ecclesiastical authority must be sub-

[1] See 'Church and Intercommunion', by W. Manson, *S.J.T.*, 4, pp. 29ff.

ordinated to the Real Presence of the Lord in the midst. And He invites whom He will to His own Table.

No doubt it would be a dishonour to Christ for two churches which refuse even to consider reunion to pretend together at the Lord's Table that they are one, but that applies equally to each church as it orders the Table within its own communion, so long as it holds itself apart from another. To eat the Body and drink the Blood of Christ sincerely is to resolve to act out that Communion in the Body; to engage in the eucharistic sacrifice and to echo Christ's high-priestly intercession for the oneness of the Church is to go from the Table sworn to fulfil to His desire for unity. It is altogether proper, and indeed a solemn duty, for two churches which are prepared before the face of God to seek a way to reunion, to come together without restriction at the Table of the Lord as soon as possible. To those who resolve to commit themselves to His grace and His ordering, He will surely grant through the Communion of His Body and Blood the penitence and healing in which we all stand in such great need.

(2) *In what sense is the Bishop to be regarded as a sign of the unity and continuity of the Church?* There can be no doubt that non-episcopal churches must give far more serious consideration to the episcopate as the universal sign of the Church's unity in space and time. If the 'historic episcopate' has been for the most part the sign throughout the ages of Church history of the oneness of the Church in Christ, then for ecumenical reasons alone every church ought to be ready for mutual adaptation with another church involving the integration of the episcopate with its appointed ministry of the Word and Sacraments. The episcopate is thus to be regarded not only as a universal sign, but as an essential sign of the Church's unity.

On the other hand, we have to ask, What is the relation between sign and thing signified with reference to the episcopate? The thing signified is surely the corporate priesthood of the whole Body and the corporate ministry of the Word and Sacrament. Is the bishop an *effectual* sign of that? Some Anglo-Catholics would affirm that he is. But is that not to make the bishop a Sacrament in precisely the same sense that the Eucharist is a Sacrament? Dare we do that? No doubt the episcopate is to be given the signification of a sign within the Church which is sacramentally incorporated into Christ as His Body, and in that sense we can speak of it as 'of a sacramental nature' like ordination to the ministry of Word and Sacrament. To go beyond that, and to make the bishop 'an effectual sign' of the unity and continuity of the Church and thus to give him independent significance in the role of a mediator, is surely not only to introduce disorder into the unity of Baptism and Eucharist, but to insist that the episcopal succession *per se* constitutes the very nature of the Church and is creative of it from age to age. That is to make the episcopate usurp the office of the One Mediator and to give it precedence over the Church which is His Body.

That is precisely the great danger, for it was that doctrine enunciated by the Tractarians making the episcopate the sole sign and guarantee of the unity and continuity of the Church which led to the inversion of the whole New Testament conception of the Church and ministry as grounded in the Body of Christ, as Dr J. A. T. Robinson has made so clear (op. cit., p. 15). Moreover it has tended increasingly to sever the hierarchy from the people and to isolate the episcopate from the corporate priesthood of the Church.

The time has surely come to reverse that tendency and seek a fuller integration of the episcopate with the presbyterate in the ministry of Word and Sacrament and an integration of the whole Church in the eucharistic fellowship. In the words of Ignatius to the Philadelphians (4.1): 'Be careful to use one Eucharist (for there is one flesh of our Lord Jesus Christ, and one cup for union with His blood, one altar, as there is one bishop together with the presbytery and the deacons my fellow-servants), in order that whatever you do you may do it according unto God.' Certainly the time has come for a proper reunion of the churches on a Biblical and doctrinal basis and in a plenitude of faith and order in which no church will be the poorer but in which all churches will be enriched.